❖

THE
GUEST
CHILDREN

❖

❖

THE
GUEST
CHILDREN

❖

The Story of the British Child Evacuees Sent
to Canada During World War II

Geoffrey Bilson

Fifth House
Saskatoon
1988

Canadian Cataloguing in Publication Data

Bilson, Geoffrey

The guest children
ISBN 0-920079-42-3

1. World War, 1939-1945 — Children — Great Britain.
2. World War, 1939-1945 — Evacuation of civilians — Great Britain.
3. World War, 1939-1945 — Evacuation of civilians — Canada.
4. World War 1939-1945 — Children — Canada. I. Title.

D809.C3B54 1988 940.53'161'0941   C88-098146-6

With the support of: The Canada Council
                     The Saskatchewan Arts Board

Published by: Fifth House
              Suite One
              128 Second Avenue North
              Saskatoon, Saskatchewan
              Canada S7K 2B2

Printed in Canada

Cover Design: Robert Grey
Cover Illustration: York University Archives
                    (Toronto Telegram Collection)

F O R E W O R D

Before his death in the summer of 1987, Geoffrey Bilson had published four books which established him as a respected social historian (*A Darkened House: Cholera in Nineteenth Century Canada*) and as a distinguished author of historical novels for children (*Goodbye Sarah, Death Over Montreal,* and *Hockeybat Harris*). Now we have occasion to celebrate the publication of a fifth work, *The Guest Children,* a social history of the evacuation of British children to Canada during World War II, their reception and settlement "for the duration."

Anyone who knew Geoffrey can understand why he was so drawn to write of the guest children. As a social historian and as an immigrant from the United Kingdom, he found the topic ideally suited to his scholarly interests and background. But what may perhaps have been even more decisive in his choice was that the novelist in him could recognize a dramatic story and how to exploit it. That is not to suggest that *The Guest Children* is not history. It is. History marked by the solid, sober, careful relating of facts and their thorough analysis. But it is also a book in which Geoffrey let the human face shine through and permitted the participants (in what for many was the great adventure of their lives) to speak for themselves in their own words. What emerges is a moving account of children torn between two worlds and two loyalties. English children, who at first cling doggedly to their "Englishness," become more and more Canadian as memories of home fade during the long war years. Children are pulled between their attachment to natural parents far over the ocean and their growing affection for, and dependence on, their foster parents, the "Aunties and Uncles" who are nearer to hand.

Perhaps the guest children's plight was a plight that only someone like Geoffrey could fully comprehend. On the one hand, I never met anyone more Canadian than he, anyone more passionately interested in the history and literature of this country. The proof of this can be found in his own contributions to both these fields. All of his histories and novels are concerned with his adopted country. Yet, like the guest children, he realized the importance of never forgetting who he was or where he came from. The last time I saw him was at a dinner he hosted in honor of the patron saint of Wales and Welsh, St. David. That day he was full of stories of his homeland and I remember him discussing, with great verve and animation, Jan Morris's book on Wales.

A writer cannot help revealing something about himself in his books. For example, *Goodbye Sarah* and *Hockeybat Harris* are indisputably the work of a man with a keen social conscience. "Hockeybat" Harris may find a secure and loving home in wartime Saskatoon but Geoffrey was careful to tell his young readers that Canada was not so welcoming to other refugees, Jews in particular. In *The Guest Children* he makes that point again. Nevertheless, what sticks in the mind about this book are the unsentimental stories of ordinary folk who were moved to make sacrifices on behalf of people they often did not know. These sacrifices were not, of course, ones commonly considered heroic. They were small, pinching, disrupting sacrifices that upset households and which were made day after day, week after week, month after month, year after year, for the sake of strangers' children.

The historian's mask of objectivity doesn't quite, I think, hide Geoffrey Bilson's admiration for this quiet decency. I am glad. Geoffrey Bilson was many things — a wit, a man of learning and culture and penetrating intelligence. Fundamentally, however, I believe he was a man to whom the old-fashioned word decent can be fairly and truly applied. It is only fitting that his last book reveals so much of that quality which Geoffrey, with typical modesty and humor, would have denied any claim to possess.

Guy Vanderhaeghe
1988

CONTENTS

CHAPTER 1

❖

THE
DOOR OPENS

❖

NINETEEN thirty-eight was a year overshadowed
by war. The Sino–Japanese War entered its
second year, the Spanish Civil War its third.
In March 1938, Hitler's armies rolled into Austria and
all summer long the news focused on the Führer's
demands on Czechoslovakia, which would be met at
Munich in September. The peace won then proved
short, and 1939 rushed toward full-scale war in Europe.
The battles fought in the 1930s brought with them the
new horror of aerial bombardment, and the
photographs of devastated homes and terrified civilians
shocked newspaper readers around the world. Military
strategists now had to wrestle with the question of how
to protect women and children living in those cities
most exposed to attack. In 1938, Britain began
planning for the evacuation of mothers and young
children from the larger cities if war broke out. By

September 1939, 1,437,000 women and children were on their way to safety in the British countryside.[1]

While the British government considered large-scale evacuation, a group of Canadian women were also thinking about the problem. In May 1938, the President of the National Council of Women, Mrs. George O. Spenser, visited Vancouver. At a garden party given by the North Shore Council of Women, she met Mrs. Emma J. Walker, who was eager to talk about the deteriorating situation in Europe. Mrs. Walker was sure that if war came it would become a war of extermination with women and children in the front line. She had already arranged to take in two young relatives if war broke out, and she suggested that the National Council think about bringing all the children of Britain to safety in Canada. Sheltered from the perils of invasion, the children would form the "nucleus of a new Britain founded on British stock." The idea caught Mrs. Spenser's imagination and she persuaded the Council executive to adopt it. In September 1939, the Council organized a National Registration of Women for war work and 100,000 women offered their homes to British evacuees.[2]

By then, others had taken up Mrs. Walker's idea. The Toronto *Globe and Mail*, which hinted that Prime Minister Mackenzie King was not warm-hearted enough in his support of Britain, appealed for aid to the children as part of its campaign against King. On July 8, 1939, it called on the government to take action. An editorial on "Our duty to British children" pointed to the horrors of air raids on civilian populations in Spain and China. Air-raid drills were now part of British life, and war would bring assaults on her cities.

Britain was too small to protect all its children by evacuation to the countryside. Canada had "done precious little on behalf of Empire defense" reasoned the *Globe*, but now it could provide a home for "Princesses Elizabeth and Margaret Rose and as many British boys and girls as we can make room for . . . we should be able to take in all those big enough to send and too young for industry or defense service."

Readers responded positively to the suggestion and the *Globe* kept up its campaign throughout the summer. Ontario Premier Mitch Hepburn endorsed the idea and seized the opportunity to maintain his own feud with King by saying that he hoped Ottawa "would not stand in the way of British children receiving a refuge in Canada from European war horrors." The Rotarians of Lindsay, Ontario, voted to make Rotary clubs clearing houses for the children. Lady Eaton offered an estate to house British evacuees. Sir Edward Beatty, president of the CPR, was quoted as saying that with careful planning the children could be moved quickly to Canada. Sir Edward obviously did not convince Prime Minister King. When Dr. Manion, the Conservative Party leader, suggested that Canada should bring over British children King replied that Britain thought it would be impossible to arrange.

When Britain declared war, on September 3, 1939, still more Canadians demanded action. Reverend H.H. Marsh, an Anglican priest in Toronto, wrote to the Immigration Branch that "one of the finest things Canada could do for the Empire in their time of crisis would be to bring to our safe shores some of the children of England or of those refugee children within her borders," and he offered to take in two to join his own two children. The network of connections between Britain and Canada came into play. Relatives wrote to ask for a home for their children or to offer to look after nephews and nieces for the duration. Businesses with branches in Canada and Britain, service clubs, churches, university professors, lawyers, doctors, dentists and other professionals all began to talk of finding homes for British children. As the war began, the English-language press wrote often of Canada's role in the Empire, an idea which still had force for many Canadians.[3]

Few Canadians took the Empire and the Commonwealth of Nations as seriously as Major Fred J. Ney, Executive Vice-president of the National Council of Education of Canada. Through that organization, and the Overseas Education League, Ney had arranged exchanges of teachers and school children between Commonwealth countries for thirty years. When war broke out, Ney had a number of British school parties travelling in Canada, including the cricket team from Roedean, an exclusive girls' school. He sent some of the children home, but a number remained in Canada and were enrolled in Canadian private schools. Ney saw the war as an opportunity to push forward his own vision of the Commonwealth. In December 1939, he wrote: "all that for which we fight — our cultural heritage — must not be allowed to disintegrate. . . . The Post War Empire will need the vision and the cooperative service of Youth for its own reconstruction and for the building and consolidation of the New World which must be the only true fruit of victory." Continuing exchanges between Britain and Canada would help to hold the Empire together, he argued. Others agreed that juvenile migration schemes should be reviewed to strengthen the bonds between Britain and the Dominions.[4]

Prime Minister King reacted to such appeals with his usual caution. Ever able to spot a scheme to embarrass him, he discounted the support for evacuation to Canada, saying the idea was impracticable, the need undemonstrated and the consequences imponderable. King's chief concern was not British evacuees but European refugees. Bombing was not the only horror that children faced in Europe in the 1930s, and thousands of refugees had fled from Hitler's Germany and Austria even before the war began. By 1940, there were close to nine thousand refugee children living in Britain and uncounted thousands in Europe. The League of Nations Society of Canada, with groups scattered across the country, had created the Canadian National Committee on Refugees and Victims of Political Persecution (CNCR) in October 1938. The CNCR was chaired by Senator Cairine Wilson, and it worked with a number of Jewish organizations to persuade the government to open the doors, at least a crack, to refugees. Members of the CNCR included clergymen, lawyers, professors and university presidents and principals. They were, for the most part, moderate-minded people who expected only modest changes in immigration regulations to allow a few thousand refugees into Canada. They met the opposition of King's government, which feared a political backlash in Quebec against Jewish immigration, and the implacable administration of the Immigration Branch under its director, F.C. Blair.[5]

F.C. Blair had made his career in the days after

the end of open immigration. Since 1931, Canada had effectively closed its doors to most immigrants. Blair had devoted his career to enforcing the Immigration Act, and he remained watchful and suspicious, especially of Jewish applicants, throughout his career. When the CNCR began to ask that Canada admit unaccompanied child refugees, Blair responded by arguing that even if parents were willing to send their children alone to Canada, his Branch was not prepared to split families. The real danger, as Blair wrote in one of his many memos on the topic, was that the families would not stay split: "Where we admit children . . . we admit the family. . . . If we admitted children who were not orphans we would never have any rest until we admitted the balance of their families."[6]

The CNCR lobbied for a more generous refugee policy and its arguments were supported by a number of newspapers in the summer of 1939. By concentrating on the plight of the children, the CNCR won a concession as the situation in Europe deteriorated. In July 1939, the government agreed to admit one hundred child refugees under the CNCR's sponsorship. Blair insisted that there would be no obligation to admit the children's families, and he required that the children be either from broken families or be orphans with one or both parents dead. Surviving parents had to sign a release before the child could be admitted. Refugee children were to be between the ages of three and fifteen and were to be placed in homes of their own religious faith.

Once the agreement had been made, the CNCR was sworn to keep it secret for fear that admitting even one hundred children would provoke a public reaction.

Blair, however, had ways of keeping the door closed even if King was prepared to open it a little. Almost a year after the agreement had been made, not one of the children had been admitted to Canada. Constance Hayward, Executive Director of the CNCR, was enraged by the Immigration Branch's delaying tactics. Blair had demanded a bond of $800 for each child, which the CNCR could not afford, and when he dropped that demand, he continued to ask for signed releases from the children's parents. Many of the parents, if they were still alive, were by then in Nazi camps.[7]

While Blair remained adamant in his opposition to Jewish immigration, he was scarcely more welcoming to British evacuees. He worried that opening the door to British children would also open it to refugees. Some petitioners made the error of admitting to Blair that they planned to bring both kinds of children to Canada. In October 1939, Mrs. Gordon Lennox told Blair that she hoped to bring to Canada "a considerable number of refugee children and child evacuees from London who may lose their parents by death or other causes attributable to war." Blair outlined his objections to her proposals in the course of a long interview. He pointed out that most refugees in Britain were not orphans and the Department did not believe in separating families. Blair agreed that some British children might lose a father, but he "suggested there was no particular need to consider a movement of these children at the present time." Air raids might orphan some children and Canada could consider their needs in the spring. Blair emphasized the difficulties and dangers of bringing children to Canada and suggested that it might be more useful to send food and clothes to Britain. Mrs. Lennox was referred to Charlotte Whitton, Executive Director of the Canadian Welfare Council, and shown out of the office.[8]

As long as The Phoney War continued, through the winter of 1939 and early months of 1940, King could ignore pleas to admit a large number of children to Canada. Evacuation inside Britain quickly proved unpopular with hosts and guests alike. The small towns were overwhelmed by mothers and children from industrial cities. Schools were choked with students and forced into double shifts. Sympathy for the evacuees gave way to resentment and derision, and as time passed without air raids, mothers and children began to drift back home. The awful destruction expected in the first days of war had not materialized, and the whole idea of mass evacuation was reevaluated. British planners decided that if there was bombing in the future only children would be evacuated from the cities. Overseas evacuation was not considered. As The Phoney War dragged on, few families thought of sending their children abroad; in 1939, only 253 children under the age of sixteen were sent from Britain to Canada.[9]

Then came the blitzkrieg. On April 9, 1940, the German army moved into Denmark and launched a campaign against Norway. A month later, the Germans began their assault on the Low Countries and in less than a week had occupied Holland. The British Expeditionary Force was pushed back to Dunkirk, and the evacuation of British and French troops began on May 27. Three days later, Belgium capitulated and by

8

early June the Germans were advancing into France. On June 16, the French began to negotiate for an armistice, which was soon signed. It seemed only a matter of days before Britain could expect an invasion; the bombing that had been feared in September began in earnest in the summer of 1940. Once more, children left the cities for the countryside, while thousands of refugees made their way from Europe to the relative safety of Britain.

The blitzkrieg shattered morale. Suddenly, the idea of sending children overseas made sense to many parents, and a scramble began among those who could afford to book passages for their children. In London, Canada House was besieged by applications for entry into Canada. On May 19, the diplomat Charles Ritchie noted in his diary that Canada House was "being invaded by women of the aristocracy wanting to send their children overseas . . . they are all looking to Canada now. We are to provide them with men and ammunition, take their children, intern their fifth column etc." The collapse and surrender of France intensified the panic. On June 22, Ritchie wrote: "Several exhausting days during which the office has been flooded with people trying to arrange for their children to get out to Canada." Later, he reflected that "Here we have a whole social system on the run, wave after wave after wave of refugees and these are only the people at the top, people who can by titles, letters of introduction, or the ruling manner force their way into Government offices and oblige one to give them an interview. What of the massed misery that cannot escape?"[10]

In 1939, 253 children had been sent privately to

Canada, but nearly 5,500 would go in 1940. Leading the rush in May and June were the children of the aristocracy and the upper classes, who had the contacts and the financial resources to meet any requirement laid down by Immigration regulations. Through the summer, cousins of Princess Elizabeth, children of Cabinet ministers and prominent journalists and intellectuals left for Canada and the United States. The King, however, rejected any suggestion that the Princesses leave. Clementine Churchill personally intervened to bar the departure of one of her great-nieces when she learned that the child was leaving Britain with her school. Neither Clementine nor Winston Churchill approved of the flight from Britain. Fifteen hundred women left Britain for Canada with their children that summer, and many of them took Nanny along to help care for the family. The British government limited exit visas to nannies who had "been in service with the family for many years" and allowed only women over sixty to be hired for new positions. On July 13, the *Globe and Mail* reported that two thousand first-class passengers had arrived that day in Canada.

Following the private evacuees came children whose parents had a harder time raising the necessary money and who had fewer contacts in Canada. As the evacuation escalated, people who had talked of evacuation in 1939 went into action. Ethnic links were developed. Rupert Davies of the Kingston *Whig-Standard* and Sir Robert Webber of the *Western Mail*, which was published in Cardiff, began work on a scheme to find homes for Welsh children in Welsh-Canadian homes. Individuals offered to sponsor children. Mrs. Angela

Bruce, wife of a former Lieutenant-Governor of Ontario, asked Lady Tweedsmuir to find one hundred children and send them over. W.R. Campbell, President of Ford of Canada, sponsored 102 children of British Ford employees and gave some of them a home with his own family. Corporations, such as C.I.L. and Kodak, service clubs — in particular Rotary — and various societies (including the Eugenics Society) brought their colleagues' children to Canada.

The University of Toronto Women's War Service Committee launched a private evacuation scheme. Founded in September 1939, the committee had established a subcommittee for refugees at an early meeting. When the war in Western Europe began, committee members contacted friends at the Universities of Birmingham, Manchester, Oxford and Cambridge. The day France surrendered, the committee decided to invite the universities to send children of their staff to Toronto. Two days later, a canvass of Toronto faculty produced 147 offers of free homes and fifty-one offers of financial help. By July 9, Toronto faculty were already caring for sixteen children from Oxford and preparing for the arrival of seventy-four children from Cambridge. The committee also helped large parties of mothers and children passing through Canada on their way to homes with faculty at Harvard and Yale. The committee's work would last until some years after the war ended in 1945.[11]

Hundreds of children went to Canada with their private schools. A correspondent wrote to *The Times* welcoming the evacuation of private schools because "the Dominions are at least as much in need of men and women turned out by our public schools as of agricultural workers." Major Ney had no doubt about the value of such arrangements. The Headmasters and Headmistresses Association of Canada announced, toward the end of June, that its members "were willing at once and during the coming school year to look after as many boys and girls from Britain as their schools can hold and the schools will do everything in their power to facilitate the transfer of children." By the time that invitation was published, Ney had sent three hundred children on their way to Canada and had one thousand more ready to leave as soon as space was available on ships. Ney used his longstanding contacts to put British and Canadian schools in touch with each other. He also had some influence with Canadian High Commissioner Vincent Massey, who agreed that the National Council of Education would act as the clearing house for schools wishing to make contact with one another.[12]

Ney, however, tended to ignore potential problems. In his contacts with the British Parliamentary Under Secretary for Dominions Affairs, Geoffrey Shakespeare, he left the impression that the Canadian government was actively interested in the school movement. On July 3, Shakespeare told the House of Commons that the Canadian government had invited schools with links in Canada to evacuate and had agreed to maintain and educate the children. Their parents would be asked to pay their fees into a trust fund in the United Kingdom. This was sheer fantasy. At the time Shakespeare made the statement, the Canadian immigration authorities did not even know that school children were already at sea. As Blair remarked, "Something may have taken place between Mr. Massey in London and the Hon. Mr. Shakespeare of which we have no record." If it did, Ney probably had a role in it. Blair later commented, "There is a great deal of fog about how some of these private school children were recruited and transferred . . . but for the most part they appear to have moved on representations made by Major Ney who seems to have represented mainly himself in giving assurance that children would be looked after by Private schools in Canada." Problems soon arose for the more than four hundred children who came to Canada with their schools in June and July.[13]

The private evacuation quickly provoked resentment in Britain. The sight of thousands of well-to-do women and children leaving Britain in the face of military disaster angered many. Forty years later, that anger still colored the memories of a fireman who was on board one of the ships to Canada:

> Well, there were kids and a lot of Army dodgers among them . . . I seen the so-called kids. Short trouser on of a day and long trouser a night on deck. They were all the richmen's sons. Lords', Dukes', Bank managers' children. I came up out of the Engine Room and my face and hands were black with the dirty job I done. There were three of your so-call[ed] children seen me and said Arn't you dirty. I said 'F off and go back and fight for your country.' They run. . . . My sisters lost a lad each in the forces; they didn't run away.[14]

The Treasury and the Bank of England expressed concern about the effect a large evacuation could have on Britain's dollar reserves. By June 1940, those reserves were rapidly shrinking and exchange controls were stringently enforced to protect what remained. The Treasury allowed each traveler to take only £10 out of the country. Transfers of funds to Canada were banned and people with assets in Canada had to remit the proceeds to London. The Treasury forbade private arrangements to pay off loans at a later date from funds in Britain. Canadian friends could no longer agree to lend money to British mothers and their children on the understanding that they would be repaid after the war. Nothing budged the Treasury from its stance. Letters from the Governor-General to a friend at Buckingham Palace asking him to "put in a word in the right quarters to ease the . . . situation," appeals by Vincent Massey and intervention by R.B. Bennett, the former Prime Minister now retired to London, were all equally unavailing.

Vincent Massey was sure that the refusal to change the regulations was "largely political as they are apprehensive that relaxation of the Treasury Regulations as proposed would appear to give privilege to well-to-do classes." He was correct. Early in July, O.D. Skelton, at External Affairs in Ottawa, had a long telephone conversation with an official of the Bank of England who was "quite exercised" over the refugee problem. He had heard that some people were arriving in Canada with more sterling than they were permitted to take out of Britain, and he was pleased to learn that Canada enforced British treasury regulations. The question "is a red-hot political mess" he told Skelton, and the Bank was determined not to allow "a privileged class of refugees."[15]

The regulations did slow the movement of private schools to Canada and made life difficult for private evacuees. But short of banning evacuation, the only way to show that it was not a privilege for the few was to make it possible for the many. As soon as the blitzkrieg began, the government in Canada came under pressure to do just that. T.A. Crerar, the Minister responsible for the Immigration Branch, was peppered in the House of Commons with questions about the government's plans to help relieve the Mother Country of the burden of caring for refugees and for offering shelter to British children. The government had no plans, and Crerar could only reply that discussions were being held with the British government. Crerar was personally concerned by the question and raised it in the War Cabinet as early as May 24.

But Crerar did not have the full respect of his Prime Minister, who thought he was "losing his grip," and he had little power in the government. His presentation to the Cabinet tended to confirm King's opinion. King noted in his diary that Crerar "had a telegram of appalling length, very muddled in thought and expression, which he read. I openly opposed the sending of it, as being too wide-open and undertaking too much in the way of government obligation." Crerar proposed that Canada should pay the cost of transporting 10,000 children from Britain and find them homes with Canadian families. Crerar's costing was vague and the Minister of Finance immediately objected. The Cabinet was not impressed by Crerar's argument that it would be a popular move and one which would help Britain. After some discussion, however, the members agreed that a limited number of places might be offered. They told Crerar to ask Britain for information about the number of children it wanted to send and to open discussions with the provinces. King noted in his diary that "we cannot refrain from sharing the burden of the democracies in Europe in taking refugees, especially children. I urged the most immediate steps or assistance be given to relieve France and England of refugees . . . What [Crerar] should do is immediately to get expert staff of persons to assist in this branch of work alone. At each stage, however, we run up against Ralston's fears as to expenditure which all these things occasion." Crerar was sent away to do his homework.[16]

Crerar soon had cables on the way to Vincent Massey reporting "strong interest" in refugee children, claiming that "at least several thousand" would find homes in Canada. He asked for information on the numbers, age range and racial origins of the refugee children in Britain. A separate cable asked Massey for his views on "the evacuation of British children to Canada." Crerar's Director of Immigration did not share his Minister's enthusiasm for such schemes. "It would be a great mistake," Blair noted on May 28, "to start on any refugee campaign that had as its spearhead the movement to the country of probably 8,000 young Jews of German nationality most of whom are partially absorbed in England." The thousands of refugees from Holland, Belgium and France were, however, "just the sort we could help and who could be placed in private homes throughout the Dominion."[17]

Within a week of his presentation to the Cabinet, Crerar announced that a conference would be held with provincial authorities to plan the reception of child refugees from Britain and France. *The Times*, of London, reported that there was "much support throughout Canada for the proposal to offer sanctuary to European refugees on a generous scale" and that newspapers, governments and public bodies were urging the government to act. A month of frantic activity on both sides of the Atlantic began on May 31. In London, negotiations opened at the Dominions office between a British group, headed by Geoffrey Shakespeare, and five men from the Canadian High Commission, headed by Lester B. Pearson. Pearson said that Canada was prepared to arrange the immediate movement to Canada of "at least several thousand refugee children from the Continent at present residing in the United Kingdom." Their passages would be paid from funds raised by an appeal in Canada and the children would be placed in private homes and supervised by provincial welfare agencies. British evacuee children were welcome to take part in this movement.

Pearson, speaking for the Department of External Affairs, applied the term refugee to any child fleeing the war. W.R. Little, speaking for the Immigration Branch, did not. In the course of the negotiations, Commissioner Little made an important distinction between refugees and evacuees. European refugee children would be admitted as immigrants; but "in view of the immediate emergency" Canada would "waive temporarily certain restrictions imposed by Immigrant status" for British child evacuees and their mothers.

Financial and medical requirements, for example, would be eased. No one appears to have asked why the emergency was more immediate for evacuees than for refugees, or to have questioned this distinction. Shakespeare, unaware that the Immigration Branch had just effectively shut out refugees, said that "a house-to-house canvass of refugee billets" would be made to find out their number and asked if Canada put a higher priority on refugees or evacuees. The British wanted to avoid the problems they had run into with home evacuation, and they asked Pearson for the information they needed to plan the move. They wanted to know if Canada preferred children of certain ages. Shakespeare asked for details of costs and payments and pointed out that Britain would prefer to remove enemy alien internees and prisoners of war from the country before space was found on ships for children. Would Canada take the internees? Canada's first response was to refuse, but after repeated requests, King finally agreed to accept both groups. Meanwhile, the various levels of government in Canada decided what kind of children would be welcome. On June 8, Massey learned that Canada preferred unaccompanied children, medically fit, 75% of them British and non Roman Catholic. Few free homes could be found for mothers with children or children under five. Most provinces preferred children at least ten years of age.[18]

The relaxed regulations made possible the large-scale private evacuation in the summer of 1940, which in turn increased the demand for government action in Britain. Canada's offer of homes, which had been followed by similar offers from Australia, New Zealand, South Africa and a private citizens' committee in the

U.S.A., could not be ignored as criticism steadily mounted against private evacuation. Geoffrey Shakespeare, a middle-ranking politician with a career of modest achievement behind him, was instructed to plan a government-sponsored evacuation. Shakespeare now made overseas evacuation his own project and threw himself into it wholeheartedly. The experience brought him great personal satisfaction but did him little political good. In 1942, he was dropped in a government shuffle.

Shakespeare's planning committee spent ten days discussing the scheme and preparing its report. The committee tried to put evacuation in a positive light by arguing that it would be a valuable experience for the children and would "reinforce close and traditional ties" between Britain and the host countries. A government scheme, in conjunction with private evacuation, would send a "proper cross section of the child population" (including Allied refugees) overseas and thus end the complaints of privilege. The children would be chosen from families, not from institutions, although children from boarding schools could apply. There had been too many objections in Canada and other countries to the export of children from British orphanages in the early years of the century to risk sending out a new generation of home boys and girls. The committee suggested that a Children's Overseas Reception Board (CORB) should run the scheme. The report was ready to be presented to the Cabinet on Monday, June 17. That Monday, however, was the worst day of the war so far, and Churchill was in no mood to talk with a minor government member about a scheme to evacuate children overseas. Even as

Shakespeare finished his presentation, a messenger came into the Cabinet Room with a paper for the Prime Minister. There was a pause while he read it, and Churchill then looked up and told his colleagues that a cease-fire had just gone into effect in France. It was the last step to the Armistice and French surrender. The Cabinet told Shakespeare to get started, dismissed him, and turned to work of greater urgency.[19]

Shakespeare left Downing Street to return to his office and begin organizing CORB. By Monday evening, he had advised the Dominion High Commissioners that the scheme would go ahead, had invited a number of politicians, civil servants and trade unionists to join the Board and had hired a staff, including Marjorie Maxse from Conservative Party Headquarters who took charge of the welfare section of CORB. Maxse would be at the heart of the daily work of CORB until the end of the war. The next day, Shakespeare called a conference of representatives from organizations like the Salvation Army and Dr. Barnado's Homes, which had long experience with sending British children overseas. A CORB representative was named in each host country and the Board of Education was asked to announce the scheme in the state schools and invite parents to apply. Late on Tuesday, Shakespeare called a press conference to announce that CORB would begin to receive applications on Thursday morning from parents whose children were in private schools. Wednesday saw the CORB staff, seconded from different government departments, setting up their office in premises requisitioned, appropriately enough, from Thomas

Cook in Berkeley Street. The travel agency's staff moved out as CORB moved in, and the offices were still in chaos when the staff quit work on Wednesday night.

The coincidence of the announcement of CORB with the fall of France produced a response no one had anticipated. When the staff arrived for work at 8 a.m. on Thursday morning, anxious parents were already waiting. An hour later, members of the Advisory Committee had to push their way through the crowd to get into the building for their meeting. By mid-morning, the police had to be called to keep order as the queue spread down the street. Another large crowd gathered outside the passport office, where parents queued for their children's passports. The journalist Vera Brittain was sure that the government had announced the scheme only because it feared for the future of the country. It was the very response Churchill had resisted when he reminded people after the Norway campaign and Dunkirk that wars are not won by evacuation.[20]

Nothing had prepared Shakespeare and CORB for this mood of desperation. The staff worked for three consecutive twelve-hour days to handle the first applications. Personal registration was cut off by the weekend. Mail applications had begun to arrive with the later morning deliveries on Thursday and the volume swelled rapidly. CORB took on a night staff to open and sort the mail, but every day built up a backlog. By the end of June, CORB employed 620 people but still could not keep pace with the work. On July 4, registrations were suspended with 211,000 children on the books. Twelve thousand were from private schools, which meant, according to Shakespeare, that "94% were from working-class families." Out of this flood of children, CORB had to select those it thought best-suited for evacuation. Speaking in the House of Commons, Shakespeare said that "harmony with the Dominions" required that CORB choose only "allied boys and girls not . . . German Jewish refugees." Refugees were rarely referred to as boys and girls.

Each Dominion government had its own requirement for harmony. Australia wanted no more than 10% Jewish children, South Africa would accept Jewish children only if they were nominated to particular homes and Canada "intimated that the proportion should be small since very large numbers of private refugee Jewish children have already reached this country." CORB sent twelve Jewish children among the 1,148 evacuees in the first four parties to Canada. "Colored children" were excluded from the scheme at the request of the host countries. Most host governments did relax the health standards for evacuees, but every parent had to certify to CORB that there was "no insanity, feeble-mindedness or epilepsy in the child's family and that the child has never suffered from fits or epilepsy." Not all parents told the truth. CORB asked for a medical certificate from the school doctor and a conduct report from the school. All children were medically examined before they boarded the ships.[21]

The New Statesman, a British journal, argued that it was "a point of national honor" to include German and Austrian children in the scheme, but went on to say that "even greater precautions should be taken to ensure that the evacuation does not create class suspicions." As part of its selection process, CORB divided applications by type of school. "A" children attended state schools, "B" children private schools. The "A" children were given a free passage, the "B" children were asked to pay a reduced fare of £15 for the passage to Canada. Parents who registered their children with CORB were told that they would be expected to make weekly payments. The charge for children on the A list was six to nine shillings a week, according to the family income; parents of children on the B list paid one pound a week. Parents assumed that the money would go, as it did in Britain, to the families taking their children. When children were nominated to friends and relations, parents were especially anxious that the money be paid directly to the families concerned.

Children who passed the tests of race, religion, health and conduct and who lived in areas given the highest priority for evacuation formed the pool from which the sailing parties were drawn. Those parties were, according to Maxse, balanced by religion, sex, age and type of school to ensure "a proportion of B children equal to the ratio of children attending private schools," which was 25% in England and Wales. As it turned out, however, only 2% of the children evacuated by CORB came from the B lists. CORB officials noted the difference without investigating the reasons. It seems probable that in reviewing the applications and approving children for evacuation, CORB's overworked staff were more likely to deal with one of the 199,746 A applications than one of the 11,702 B applications. The work of selecting the children and interviewing the 19,000 applicants for positions as escorts dragged on slowly in the summer of 1940 and by October only 24,474 of the 211,000 children had been approved for evacuation.[22]

The British Cabinet was not sorry to see the selection go so slowly. The stunning response to the scheme forced a cutoff of registrations, but the problems involved in moving the 200,000 children who had been registered were disturbing enough. Shakespeare claimed that he was "warned through a High Treasury Official" that if he forced the pace of CORB evacuation the Cabinet might decide to end it altogether. A mass evacuation raised questions of money, morale and priorities. The government announced that only a limited scheme was intended, and it put such a low priority on child evacuation that Shakespeare found it difficult to obtain space for the children on transatlantic ships. The Cabinet preferred to use what space there was for the internees and prisoners of war. In June, the Ministry of Shipping agreed to send evacuees on returning troopships, but it told Shakespeare that the space might be required for internees. Shakespeare had also decided that safety required the children to travel in convoys under escort rather than on unconvoyed fast liners. This decision, which proved wise, further limited his choice. Mounting criticism of the delay in sending the children to safety troubled Shakespeare, and he was relieved when he was able to advise Canada that the first children would sail early in July. T.A. Crerar trumpeted the news in the Canadian House of Commons, and the British Admiralty promptly canceled the plans because of the security leak.[23]

Shortly after the cancellation, the *Arandora Star*, a fast, unescorted liner, was torpedoed off the Irish coast. It sank in half an hour with great loss of life. Many of the passengers were internees and prisoners of war and rumor said that they had been substituted for evacuees at the last moment. The disaster led the British Cabinet to order CORB to send children to sea only in convoyed vessels, which confirmed the decision already taken by Shakespeare. Once more, CORB began to book berths for the children only to have the plans canceled when the War Cabinet decided that it could not spare Royal Navy ships to escort convoys to Canada. Asked to comment on the second cancellation, F.C. Blair said that it would "come as a great disappointment throughout Canada."[24]

Some members of the Labour Party in Britain were not only disappointed but also suspicious and angry. When Clement Attlee announced the decision in the House of Commons on July 16, he provoked a barrage of complaints from members of his own party. One Labour member said, to cheers, that the whole CORB scheme had been mere "camouflage" for private evacuation. Another expressed the fear "commonly held in the country that now that some thousands of rich people's children had gone overseas there was to be no opportunity for the children in the elementary schools." James Griffiths said that the children of the rich should be the last to leave and that if the scheme did not take children from all kinds of homes, the rich should not be allowed to go. He denounced cabinet ministers who had sent their children abroad and concluded, "After all, this is old, class-ridden Britain." George Tomlinson attacked Duff Cooper, the Minister of Information, for calling on men in public office to build the nation's confidence while he lacked "confidence in its powers to defend his own children." To this torrent Shakespeare could only reply somewhat feebly that his government colleagues and M.P.s "only took the opportunity of sending their children to safety when the Government's scheme gave workers' children the same chance."

The debate in the House of Commons finally led Churchill to make public his feelings on the question of evacuation. A few days earlier, he had responded privately to a letter from an eleven-year-old boy published in *The Times*. The boy wrote to his parents:

> [I] beg you not to let me go to Canada (I suppose you know that we are probably going?) A) Because I don't want to leave Britain in time of war. B) Because I should be very homesick. I am feeling likewise now. C) Because it would be kinder to let me be killed with you . . . than to allow me to drift to strangers and finish my happy childhood in a contrary fashion. D) I would not see you for an indefinite time, perhaps never again. Letters would simply redouble my homesickness. P.S. I would rather be bombed to fragments than leave England.

The letter was shown to Churchill and he learned that the author was David Wedgwood Benn, the youngest son of a prominent Labour M.P. Churchill wrote at once to congratulate the boy's father for Benn's "splendid letter . . . We must all try to live up to this standard," and he sent David Wedgwood Benn an autographed copy of *My Early Life* for which he received an enthusiastic thank-you note that ended, "I am very glad that I am not to be ushered into safety."

It was this spirit Churchill invoked when he rose in the House on July 18 to speak on evacuation. The Prime Minister said it was "most undesirable that anything in the nature of a large-scale exodus from this country should take place." He thanked the Dominions for their invitations but argued that there was no military need for large-scale evacuation and no physical capacity to carry it out. He turned to the criticism made a few days before to say that future sailings would be small and dedicated to "restoring the balance between the classes . . . there shall be no question of rich people having an advantage, if advantage there be, over poor." Churchill ended by admitting "frankly . . . the full bearings of this question were not appreciated by His Majesty's Government at the time when it was first raised." They did not foresee that "it would lead to a movement of such dimensions and that a crop of alarmist and depressing rumors would follow at its tail, detrimental to the interest of national defense." Churchill would happily have halted the entire scheme, but that was politically difficult to do in July 1940, and he had to be content with seeing the exodus checked and delayed by shipping problems. After weeks of delay, the first party of eighty-six CORB children left for Canada late in July and on July 30 a second party of 165 followed. Churchill had his last word on the subject when the Home Secretary was impolitic enough to suggest that a child in the first party should carry a message from Churchill to Mackenzie King. Back came the Prime Ministerial minute: "I certainly do not propose to send a message by the senior child to Mr. Mackenzie King, or by the junior child either. If I sent any message by anyone, it would be that I entirely deprecate any stampede from this country at the present time."[25]

The Canadian government had its own problems with the evacuation in the summer of 1940. Many of the private evacuees ran out of money soon after their arrival when the British Treasury changed its rules. Blair told a reporter on July 19 that seven hundred evacuees were stranded in Canada because their sponsors were not standing up to their responsibilities. Blair's figure had little connection to the facts. Most British mothers managed to support themselves and their children with the help of friends and relatives and by going to work. Blair, however, seized the opportunity to order steamship companies not to carry "any women" until the Immigration Branch was sure that satisfactory arrangements had been made for them in Canada.[26]

There was also reason to worry about the private schools. The National Council of Education had claimed to have "unlimited" offers of hospitality which made it "able to assist any school which cares to avail itself of our . . . contacts in the Dominion." In fact, the offers were limited. Many of the Canadian schools had space for British children because their own enrollments had fallen during the Depression. Falling enrollments, however, had left them short of money. Very few schools could afford to take in children for a long period of time without payment. On July 16, Blair told Ney that "his work had brought many protests," and that Massey had been told to stop transferring residential schools to Canada. The open-door policy had led to children being "figuratively turned adrift or made a charge upon private charity." Ney was told to settle the problems of the four hundred children he had already brought to Canada before bringing any more. If he could not, the "student movement will stop immediately." Ney replied that "ample hospitality" was available for the children but, by the end of July, even he had to agree that there were problems.

Money troubles slowed the movement of private school children to Canada, although the National Council of Education was still planning the transfer of small groups when evacuation ended in October. Meanwhile, the host schools in Canada scrambled to find funds from friends, alumni and community sponsors to pay for the British children. When Ney was forced to telegraph Edgehill School in Windsor, N.S., to offer to "scatter the group" of Roedean girls he had placed there (since no funds were available for them), Edgehill School found money for the girls' fees. R.B. Bennett paid the expenses of Sherborne School. Schools that tried to maintain a separate identity sometimes had great difficulties. At Lady Eden's school, which spent most of the war years in a small town in Quebec, older girls did the household chores and were even pressed into service to teach the younger children. Pembury Grove was disbanded in December 1941, when its headmistress fell ill with ulcers brought on by the strain and "indignity" of borrowing money without being able to say when it would be repaid.[27]

As the number of private evacuees entering Canada grew, the government came under increasing criticism for delays in bringing over the government-sponsored evacuees. Lengthy negotiations with the provinces in June prepared the way, but King's critics wanted to see thousands of refugees arriving in Canada. The higher priority given to internees and prisoners of war, the cancellation of voyages and the temporary suspension of the scheme all originated in London, but those people in and out of Parliament who felt that King was not doing enough to support Britain seized on the delays to attack him on the refugee question. T.A. Crerar faced many questions in June about the speed of evacuation and the numbers that would be coming. It was this harassment which led him to announce the first CORB sailing in July and caused the British to cancel it. There was no doubt that the British children were eagerly awaited.

Then, in July, the CORB children began their journey. Called "Seavacuees" by the British newspapers, they came from the cities of Britain that were being blitzed or that lay under the flight paths of the bombers or across the invasion routes the Germans would follow. Middlesborough, Newcastle, Colchester, Liverpool and London were among the first cities to send CORB children to Canada. The selection process weeded out desperately poor children to avoid the cultural difficulties that had marked the home evacuation, but some of the CORB children came from homes where money was short. They were allowed to take only what would fit into one suitcase, but a final check at the port showed that some children could not fill even the single bag. Sir Simon Marks, of Marks and Spencer, offered up to £7,500 of clothing to complete the outfits of CORB children. With Sir Simon's help, a CORB boy might travel equipped with one cap, one suit, one pair of gray pants, three pairs of socks, one sleeveless sweater, one pullover, three shirts, four vests, one dressing gown, one overcoat, one mac, one pair of trunks, one pair of shoes, one pair of running shoes, two pairs of pajamas, two pairs of shorts, one Bible, six handkerchiefs, one face cloth, one towel and one toothbrush.[28]

Within days, and sometimes hours, of hearing the news that they were off to Canada, the children were on their way to the local railway station. Many CORB children were taking the first train ride of their lives. The novelty and excitement overcame some children's anxieties when the moment came to leave. Seven-year-old Mary "said goodbye without tears, waved enthusiastically as the train drew out and indeed was reported still to be waving from the window at the next station." "Other kids were crying and screaming they didn't want to go and I was bouncing on the seat saying, 'When does the train go, Mum? I want to see the Mounties.'" A young girl who had been told it was "unbritish" to cry waved goodbye, and then joined the other children singing "There'll always be an England."

Parents were struck by a sudden sense of loss as the children clambered onto buses and trains amid the singing and excitement. Elaine never forgot the sight of her father "standing on the platform in his Anthony Eden hat and crying." One mother recorded the pain she felt at the moment of parting: "As the train was on the point of going I said to them, 'Come on, jump out and come back with Mummy. We will find a cottage somewhere where old Hitler won't find us.' But no, he just said, 'Now don't you dare cry Mummy or you will make us. Then the teachers will think we are babies.'"

Parents returned to their empty houses and the uncertainty of wondering if they had made the right decision. One mother told her children's foster mother: "I still try not to think of the last two days that they were with me as it still hurts terribly . . . both broke down at meal times and just had to have a cry, and of course all my own bravado went as well just for a little while; we tried to keep it up, each for the other's sake . . . I feel I miss the children more every day." Another wrote: "I shall never forget the first few days, the terrible emptiness in my home and seeing their little school pals . . . inquiring after them. Their bedrooms and toys, everything seemed to remind me of them. I thought I should go crazy." This separation, as intense as a bereavement, opened a gap between some parents and children that would never close.[29]

The trains rattled through the countryside, carrying the children to Liverpool or Glasgow, which were the exits to Canada. CORB children usually spent a few days bedded down in empty schools or colleges while other children in their party arrived from all over the country. The nights were broken by air-raid warnings and falling bombs. Often, at night, the children were taken into basements for shelter as bombs shook the buildings. Once in port, the evacuees were divided into parties of fifteen; they met their escorts for the voyage, were issued with their CORB identity disks — paper disks in plastic covers that soon began to disintegrate in the hands of curious children — and received medical examinations. The smaller children were put in charge of older ones appointed as prefects — although as one of these seniors noted in his diary, "Candidly, we made as much racket as the others." The long days of waiting proved too much for some children, who were rumored to have been sent back with homesickness.[30]

The delays in port were the unavoidable ones of wartime, as ships were sunk, damaged or diverted to more urgent tasks by the Ministry of Shipping or the Admiralty. When at last a vessel appeared, the children were hurried on board. Geoffrey Shakespeare tried to see each party off and "heroically kissed some hundreds before they left England." Young Bill noted in his diary that Shakespeare was "an oldish-looking man but very agile to look at and quite jovial." Shakespeare developed a farewell speech in which he reminded the children that they were British ambassadors who "must behave even better" than they knew how. If they behaved badly, people would say: "What frightful children! Their parents in Britain really cannot be worth fighting for!" If they behaved well: "What splendid children they are! We must do everything we can to help their parents win." If things went wrong, he told them, "remember you are British and grin and bear it." Many children had cause to remember those last words during their years in Canada.[31]

CHAPTER II

❖

DOWN
TO THE STATION

❖

JOHN HUTTON: Age 7
CORB Evacuee

John lived with his grandmother and his widower father in a big old house in Colchester, Essex. His mother had died when John was five, and he was a rather anxious and lonely child. Perhaps for that reason, his father said nothing about plans to send him to Canada until it was almost time to go: "My earliest recollection of Canada is of my father arriving home one day in July 1940 and telling me I would be going off to Canada in three days. I do not remember being put out by the idea. I asked where Canada was and whether I should be able to speak the language. My Uncle Leslie, being a scholar, soon produced an atlas showing Toronto, Ontario, where I would be living. He told me that the people in that part of Canada spoke English. He also told me I should be near the Niagara Falls, which were the largest waterfalls in the world.

"Being close to the East Coast and in what appeared to be imminent danger of invasion by the German army, we already had some limited possessions ready to move, should the need arise. A year before, at the time of Munich, my father had bought rucksacks for the family as a precautionary measure. A few days after I had been told I should be going to Canada, my father took me on the top of the Colchester Corporation double-decker bus, to the North Station to join a train with some other children for the first stage of our journey, under the care of adult guides. I remember clearly my father and other parents saying goodbye through the carriage window, but do not recall that any of the children were in any way distressed as the train pulled away, whatever the feelings of those we were leaving behind. None of us had any comprehension of how long it would be before we returned home. As the train gathered speed over the viaduct at Lexden, we looked down across the Hilly Fields and over to the town and to the clock tower of the Town Hall on the horizon, with the bulky form of 'Jumbo,' the water tower, close by. I remember thinking that it might be some time before I should walk along the Hilly Fields again with my Uncle Cecil. The vision of my home town receding into the distance stayed with me throughout my five years in Canada."

The children spent days, which seemed like weeks to John, waiting in London. Meanwhile, the Battle of Britain raged overhead, and John could see the vapor trails and hear the gunfire high above. At last the word came to move, and the children travelled to Liverpool to board the *Oronsay* for the voyage to Halifax.

NINA LAVILLE: Age 11
CORB Evacuee

The war began on Nina's eleventh birthday. Living in the industrial part of Middlesborough "with two huge gasholders right at the bottom of the street," Nina's parents found it easy to picture the explosions should any bombs fall close to their neighborhood. Nina's mother wrote to her Uncle Mark, a farmer settled in Steeldale, Saskatchewan. He replied at once that he would be glad to look after his great-niece. The talk about Canada excited Nina: "I do remember *pestering* to be allowed to go to Canada." She found Saskatchewan in her atlas, but Steeldale was too small for the map. Her friends were "upset that I would be leaving, but I do remember by best friend saying '*My* mother wouldn't let me go'."

Though "not a poor family," the Lavilles could not afford private evacuation for their only child. When CORB was announced, Nina was registered and "in August I was on my way to Canada as an evacuee. The farthest I had travelled was to Redcar — about eight miles to the coast with the Sunday School Outing once a year and to visit my cousin who lived in York, all of fifty miles away." Nina joined her CORB party for the trip to Liverpool and said goodbye to her parents at Middlesborough station. "I cannot *believe* how brave I was."

DAVID BROWN: Age 8
Rotary Evacuee

David had been evacuated from his home in Edgeware, Middlesex, at the beginning of the war, and it was during a school visit by his parents in the summer of 1940 that he learned that he was going to Canada. Mr. Brown had made the arrangements through Rotary for David and his younger sister, Janette, to stay with two Rotary families in Montreal. David "had hardly heard" of Canada but he accepted his parents' decision: "Everyone was being evacuated away from zones of high risk. I recall my reaction as one of excitement. I had no sense of the dangers of staying or going."

The children travelled with their parents to Liverpool and spent a night in a hotel, where they were disturbed by air-raid warnings. The sirens convinced Mr. and Mrs. Brown that they were making the right decision as they handed their children over to Miss Hope, their escort for the journey to Montreal on the *Duchess of Richmond*.

MARY ANN WAGHORN: Age 7
CORB Evacuee

Mary Ann and her three-year-old brother lived in a "warm and happy family with a background of many aunts, uncles and cousins." It was a wrench for her mother to let her go, but life in Maidstone, Kent, was dangerous in 1940, and she agreed reluctantly that her daughter would be safer in Canada. Mary Ann "was prepared some weeks prior to departure by talk of a holiday to go and see my aunt. I have only a vague recollection of being excited at the prospect of this so-called holiday." The fact that she was leaving home for a long time did not register. Instead, Mary Ann "was bubbling over with excitement whilst waiting for the train at Maidstone West Station" one morning early in August. As soon as her mother returned to the empty house, she regretted her decision. She learned later that Mary Ann had spent two nights at a college in Eltham, a nearby town, while the party of two hundred children was assembled. Had she known how close by her daughter was, Mrs. Waghorn would have gone and "fetched me home."

The CORB party travelled to Liverpool to join the *Duchess of York*. By then, Mary Ann was confused and anxious about what was happening to her. "For some extraordinary reason I 'see' everything in shades of gray—no color at all. I recall sleeping overnight in some large hall, almost surely on the floor wrapped in blankets, and it all seemed very strange to me. By that time, many children were beginning to find it not at all to their liking! Leaving what I later found to be Liverpool, I still remember only grays and, I think, rain."

THE CURTIS FAMILY
CORB Evacuees

Mr. and Mrs. Curtis lived with their seven children in a four-bedroom terrace house in Chelmsford, Essex, where Mr. Curtis worked as a bus inspector. The children stayed in Chelmsford when the war began, but in the spring of 1940, their schooling was interrupted by air-raid warnings that sent the children ducking under their desks or hurrying into the shelters in the schoolyard. Mr. Curtis worried about their safety, and when one of the children brought home information about CORB, the family sat down to discuss who should go to Canada. They agreed the fifteen-year-old boy was too old to go and the five-year-old boy too young. Hazel, aged thirteen, agreed to go to look after the younger children, who were given no choice. Mr. Curtis registered Hazel, eleven-year-old Muriel, nine-year-old Fred, and Geoffrey and Tony, the seven-year-old twins, with CORB.

As the eldest, Hazel was "apprehensive but excited about the new 'adventure.' I think we were all young and immature — thus didn't realize the seriousness of the venture." Muriel was "very excited" but Fred can "only remember feeling rather apprehensive." The twins were glad that Hazel would be looking after them.

The Curtis children's journey began at Chelmsford station early in August. They were in the same party as Mary Ann Waghorn and spent two nights at the college at Eltham while the group assembled. Hazel worried about the younger children and "I remember being frightened in case we were parted," but Tony's only worry was looking after his gas mask, which he happily relinquished when they boarded the ship in Liverpool.

JOHN JARVIS: Age 5
CORB Evacuee

John's parents came from the south of England, but his father's job as a travelling salesman for a paint company had brought the family north before John was born. When the war began, the Jarvises were living in Southport, a pleasant seaside town a few miles outside Liverpool. By the end of 1940, Southport had become home to five hundred evacuees from London, but in the early summer, it seemed an exposed and dangerous place. No one knew which route the German invasion would take and all coastal towns appeared vulnerable. Pill boxes sprang up on the roads leading down to Southport's wide and sandy beaches. Any air raids on Liverpool put Southport at risk, and bombs fell on the town during the autumn blitz. Mrs. Jarvis thought it "wicked" to willingly keep children in the danger areas, and she worried about her relatives in London. She wrote to friends and relatives in Canada to find a home for ten-year-old Michael and his younger brother, John. A friend mentioned that her sister was willing to take two boys into her home in Grimsby, Ontario. Mrs. Jarvis wrote at once to Mrs. Foster, but had to explain that if the children went as private evacuees she could not send any money to Canada. Her plan was to follow them to Canada and find work. The day after she mailed her letter, Mrs. Jarvis heard that the boys had been chosen by CORB to join an early party. By the time she received a reply from an aunt in Calgary, who also agreed to take in the boys, they were on their way to Canada.

Mrs. Jarvis worried about sending John when he

was so young. She thought he was still a bit of a "mummy's boy" and it took her some time to "pluck up the courage to send him away." John's strong attachment to his brother helped to persuade her that it was for the best, and she consoled herself with the hope that she would soon join the boys in Canada. Mrs. Jarvis tried for months to arrange an exit visa and passage, but without success.

John was told weeks before he left Southport that he was going to Canada. He was very excited and kept asking his mother "when a boat would be ready for them." One Saturday morning, Mrs. Jarvis was told to have the boys ready to travel on Monday or Tuesday, "so we had to dash out and buy all the things we had put off getting thinking we had plenty of time." The shopping and packing were done in time to put the boys on the train early in the morning on August 6. It was a hot summer day less than two months after his fifth birthday when John left home. He travelled to Glasgow by train and spent four nights in the assembly center while children from all over Britain joined the party. At five o'clock on Saturday morning, the children were loaded into coaches and taken down to the docks to board what might have been the *Duchess of York*. By then, John was bewildered and unsure about what was happening.

BETTY HEELEY: Age 9
Rotary Evacuee

Betty and her eleven-year-old brother, Michael, lived in the small town of Holmfirth near the industrial city of Huddersfield in Yorkshire. Their father was a solicitor and their mother a full-time housewife. Nana, the children's grandmother, lived with them in a close-knit family. The house was constantly visited by friends and relatives who took a warm interest in the children. Holmfirth was in no immediate danger of being bombed, but German bombers did pass over the town. At the Air Raid Precautions report center, where Betty's father spent his nights, there was much discussion about a German invasion. In June, following the fall of France, many men agreed that the Yorkshire Moors seemed a likely spot for a German invasion by air. As the weeks passed, the war in the Atlantic began and food became scarcer. Mrs. Heeley argued that the family should stay together and take their chances, but her husband persuaded her that she was being unfair. They had had a good life, and it was only right that, if things did come to the worst in England, Betty and Michael should have the chance of a future. Reluctantly, Mrs. Heeley agreed to register the children with Rotary and wrote to two families in Windsor, Ontario. Betty would go to stay with the Hardys and Michael with the Chicks.

At first Betty thought everyone was going, and she found the whole idea "very exciting." It took her some time to realize that she and Michael would be going alone. But at least her brother would be with her, and two of her friends from Holmfirth—Paddy and Brenda—would go with them to Windsor. The four children were to travel with the wife of a local Rotarian doctor who was taking her own children to Canada. The group was soon on its way to Liverpool. Despite her parents' reassurances that this was the best decision, Betty boarded the *Duchess of Atholl* confused and unhappy. She and Michael shared a cabin, and Paddy and Brenda shared another with some grownups. The doctor's wife "disappeared," and the children were left to look after themselves once the convoy set sail on August 16.

FRED: Age 13
CORB Evacuee

Fred's father worked as a driver with the London and North Eastern Railway in Middlesborough in 1940. Fred (not his real name) was evacuated with his school when the war began and was living in a small country town when the letter came from his parents. They had decided that Fred and his younger brother would be much safer with their uncles in Manitoba. When the CORB scheme was announced, their parents registered the boys and nominated them to their relatives. In June 1940, word came that Fred and his brother would leave with one of the first parties for Canada. They were given no choice about going or staying and were sent to Canada because "it was the only country in which we had relatives."

"At first I was very excited at the prospect. Most of my friends were quite envious but wished me well. But as the time came to leave, I was very distressed and tried to change the decision." It was too late to change, and the boys were taken to Middlesborough station one summer morning for the trip to Liverpool. They stood on the platform, wearing the big CORB identity labels, and said goodbye. Everyone broke down as the boys climbed onto the train, and Fred remembered "the tearful departure" for the rest of his life. It was the start of a journey that led him to great unhappiness.

GRANIA O'BRIEN: Age 12
Lady Eden's School

Grania's family had left its home in London and moved to Hampshire when the war began. Her father joined the London Rifle Brigade and her mother planned to move with him from station to station as long as he served in Britain. Mrs. O'Brien had recently inherited her family's castle in Ireland, but she thought it a poor refuge for the children if a German invasion of England came, as she believed it would, through Ireland. Life in England looked precarious in June 1940, and Grania's parents decided overseas evacuation was the safest course for their two daughters. Captain O'Brien knew Canada from prewar fur-buying visits, but he first thought of sending the girls to Australia. The O'Briens changed their plans when they heard that a small private school in Lyndhurst was planning to evacuate to Canada. The school was run by Lady Eden, who intended to take her own five children, her sister and her three children, and any other pupils at the school who wished to go. Canada was closer to home than Australia, and Grania and Deirdre were enrolled at the school.

Grania was "excited at the adventure and quite oblivious of the fact that it might be years of separation from my family." Some of her friends took the news badly and told Grania that their parents would not send them abroad because "it would be running away."

45

She and her fifteen-year-old sister were given no choice, however, and were soon rushing to get ready for the journey. Grania wrote in her diary: "So we came down to London and got skiing suits, shoes and lots of other things. Daddy gave us each a fur coat, Deirdre a muskrat and I an ocelot cat. Mummy bought me a pair of navy blue high-heeled shoes. For the journey we were allowed one trunk, one suit-case and one holdall. Thursday, July 18th, we went to Canada House for a medical examination. We were then told the luggage had to be at Euston at half-past two. Mummy and Peli packed and were so busy that they had no lunch. A taxi came and they took the luggage to the station. We were told we had to go on the morrow but we were not told when we were to sail."

The next day, Mrs. O'Brien took the girls to Euston station where they met the school party. Grania knew some of the children in the group and she had her sister for company. The bustle of organizing the party helped to obscure the pain of leaving. Grania noted: "Then we went on the platform, got into the train, got our places, got out again, said goodbyes and kisses, got in the train again and we started at ten past eight."

The journey to Liverpool was slow, and when the train stopped at dockside there was another long delay before the party went aboard the *Duchess of Atholl*. Once on board, the girls were placed in groups and assigned to cabins. Some of the cabins were below the waterline, however, and the children were moved to share cabins on the upper decks, which meant that some spent their nights sleeping on the floor. Once the cabins had been sorted out, there was time to explore the ship, which had "three shops, a lift and lots of other things."

HAZEL WILSON: Age 14
CORB Evacuee

Hazel, her brother and her two-year-old sister lived in Colchester, where her father worked in one of the local factories. One morning, the *Daily Express* published a front-page story about the CORB scheme, and Mr. and Mrs. Wilson asked the older children if they were interested. Hazel and her brother said they were. Canada was their first choice because they felt it "was not as extreme as the U.S.A." Hazel had been sent on holidays without her parents before, and this seemed like another holiday. She felt "excited — absolutely thrilled" at the idea of going to Canada: "I didn't think of the homesickness side of it." The Wilsons registered their two oldest children with CORB and waited for word. The letter came in the early summer, "but we were warned not to let anyone know as movements were secret and we were on twenty-four hours' notice — not even our schools knew we were leaving."

Hazel did not even tell her best friend that she was going. Years later, she learned that her friend had "wondered what happened to me when I didn't show up at her house any more, so she went to my house with some goodies for me, thinking I was ill. That's when she found out I had left." By then, Hazel was in Liverpool after a "terrifying trip — all strange kids" and was spending the days at a school where the children slept every night on straw pallets while the sirens wailed and bombs fell on the city. Hazel avoided her brother in these new surroundings: "I was at the age where brothers were a drag (very immature)." The gap would widen during the years ahead in Canada.

CYNTHIA LORD: Age 11
St. Hilda's School

Cynthia's school had been evacuated at the beginning of the war, but she became so unhappy that she was allowed to return home after one term. Mr. Lord was an engineer at Bellingham-on-Tees, and the family lived in Norton-on-Tees near Middlesborough. It was a heavily industrialized part of England and an obvious target for the Germans' bombs. In June 1940, the air raids began and Cynthia's parents made plans for her evacuation. At first, they thought of sending her to stay with an aunt in Australia, but they were not sure that she would be happy living without friends of her own age.

One Wednesday in June, Mr. Lord heard that St. Hilda's School, in Whitby, Yorkshire, was planning to evacuate to Canada. He decided at once that Cynthia should go with them. "At eleven, one really couldn't be given a choice. My parents experienced fighting in the first world war and although I was consulted about it, it was put to me as a great adventure, which it was . . . at the time, [it] didn't seem any worse than going to boarding school. This would have happened to me in a year or so anyway." Cynthia's older brother was in medical school in Edinburgh, and her parents pointed out that they would be freer to carry on with their war work if they were sure Cynthia was safe. In any case, "we were all convinced that the war would be over by Christmas." Three days after Mr. Lord heard about St. Hilda's plans, Cynthia and her friend Helen were in Whitby as new girls at the school.

St. Hilda's left Whitby early in July for Liverpool.

After a night at the University, the girls boarded the *Duchess of Atholl*. The party, which filed through the crowd in a crocodile, made a great impression on parents who were saying goodbye to their own children at the dock. Shepherded by the Anglican nuns who taught at St. Hilda's, the crocodile reflected the discipline and restrictions that Cynthia already disliked in her new school.

CHAPTER III

❖

THE
DOOR CLOSES

❖

LIFE on board ship was a magical experience for most of the children. Part of the last generation of ocean travel, the *Anselm* and *Antonia*, the *Oronsay* and the *Duchesses of Richmond, of Bedford, of Atholl, of York* and the *Empress of Australia* were among the ships travelling between Canada and Britain. Some of them already carried the marks of war. On the *Oronsay*, the children were told that the clock in the main reception room had been stopped and a leg blown off the grand piano while she was helping in the evacuation at Dunkirk. All the children found the ships exciting and opulent. One boy described his as "a floating palace." The portholes were covered to prevent the light from escaping, but the ships blazed with light inside, delighting the children who had spent the nights since September 1939 in blacked-out cities.

For many, the greatest delight of all was the food.

Rationing of some foods had begun in January 1940, and non-rationed items, such as bananas, were no longer readily available in the shops. Food on the transatlantic liners was abundant. Sitting at tables decorated with fresh flowers, the children could consult the "splendid menu cards" and ask the help of "indulgent stewards who treated us like grownups." Some of the discoveries were reassuring—an eight-year-old girl was "amazed to have Kellogg's Corn Flakes—exact same food as home." But there were more exotic possibilities, and one seven-year-old boy "always asked for smoked salmon." Most of the children showed more predictable tastes: "They have ice cream for dinner most nights, the boys have two some nights." An eight-year-old wrote home cryptically: "It was very good ice creams and jellys and all sorts of things. It wasn't as good as I thought."[1]

As the ships hit the first ocean waves, however, the majority of passengers forgot about eating. "Terribly rough. I am seasick 9 times (poor me)" one girl wrote home. Safe in Canada, another girl summed up the voyage: "I enjoyed it very much even though I was sick 25 times." Sickness among the teachers and escorts reduced the discipline over the children, and even when the adults had recovered, sheer numbers allowed the children to create their own society. Twelve-year-old boys "ran riot."[2]

The ships rolled on over the Atlantic, on some voyages changing course every seven minutes to confuse German submarines. Despite the fun and freedom on board, the children seldom forgot that they were in danger. In the first days of the war, the *Athenia* had been torpedoed, leaving no doubt that passenger ships were at risk, just as they had been in the First World War. The sinking of the *Arandora Star* drove the lesson home. The routine of the voyage constantly reminded the children of the dangers they faced. Before the ships left port, the passengers held a lifeboat drill which was repeated every day. Any possibility of attack by submarines brought the children to their lifeboat stations. A party from St. Hilda's School had "nightly drills on deck" and once were "chased by submarines — the nuns did a lot of praying then." Thirteen-year-old Margot made her sister wear, as she did herself, two of everything and then filled their pockets with precious possessions: "If the ship had been hit she and I would have sunk like rocks, we were so heavy with clothing etc.!"[3]

For children travelling in convoys, there was the added excitement of watching the escort vessels. The war could come very close. After days of pleasurable excitement, nine-year-old Joyce "finally realized the seriousness of the situation when we watched one of our convoy ships sinking, the result of a German torpedo. We had to spend one day herded in the diningroom, wearing life jackets, until the danger was over."[4]

After the tension and excitements of the voyage, the happiest sight was that of land. As the ships steamed into port, the children lined the rails and sang wartime favorites like "Roll out the Barrel" and "There'll always be an England." At dockside, while people on shore waved and cheered, some of the children threw down the big English pennies they had brought with them and scrambled for the Canadian coins pitched up to them in return. Before the children disembarked, someone found the time to give each of them a New Testament.

The arrival of hundreds of children at a time put a strain on the railways, which were already stretched to find rolling stock to move troops. The CPR provided old Pullman cars to carry the children, while the CNR hauled out its old colonists' cars. Some of those cars were so ancient that the seats were propped up with pieces of lumber. No matter how ramshackle the trains, everything about them intrigued the evacuees. The porters made a big impression: "We had never seen colored people before. I was very impressed with the attendant on the train. He . . . was very kind to us all during the journey." "The Negro waiters on the train picked blueberries for us." In the colonists' cars, the CORB children slept bundled in blankets and without pillows. Train travel was dirty, too, and one girl wrote home describing the results: "You got so black though you wash and in five minutes you were just as black as before you washed. . . . We got very dirty and were continually washing our hands, necks (especially) and faces."

In fact, washing became one way to while away time on a long and tiring journey, and some children took to it enthusiastically. The cars were quickly flooded with soapy water and sodden paper towels while the children rode on as grubby as ever. On one train heading toward Saskatoon, fifty children drained a one-thousand-gallon water tank between Melville and Watrous, a distance of eighty miles. They remained so dirty that the railwaymen brought buckets of water from the commissary car to wash them before they got off for some exercise in Saskatoon. "I can assure you that trying to dry a little kiddie's face with a paper towel is not very satisfactory" one of them reported. The Red Cross began to give every child a bag with soap, towel, washcloth, books and something to while away the hours on the train — needlework kits for the girls and drawing books for the boys. Best of all, according to Keith Jopson, a CORB representative in Ottawa, was "a handkerchief bearing, in brilliant colors, a noble and romantic effigy of a trooper of the Canadian Mounted Police. As the children invariably demanded to see a 'Mountie' immediately they set foot on Canadian soil, the latter gift should prove a treasured possession." The Immigration Branch increased the number of escorts travelling with the children to help reduce some of the chaos on the cars.[5]

When they turned away from the washroom, the children gazed through the train windows at an unfamiliar landscape rolling past. They noticed "the strange shape of the farm fields" and most were impressed by the sheer size of the country and the emptiness of the land. Bill recorded that it was "very woody and no habitations. Gradually we came upon clearings with a wooden shack about the size of one ordinary room. They looked very dilapidated and liable to fall down at any moment. We have not seen many brick houses at all." One child found Canada "big, bleak and dreary" and a fifteen-year-old girl arriving in March summed it up as "so much snow and so many fir trees." Homesickness swept in with the dust and steam, and to Phyllis, "it seemed a lifetime since we had left home."[6]

The first days in Canada brought a jumble of impressions. The light of the sun blazed down by day and the streets and houses were brightly lit at night. After nearly a year of blackout the children shouted with glee at the lighted streets. Big, pastel-colored cars roamed about freely on the right-hand side of the roads. One boy was reported to have remarked: "My word, what a rotten waste of petrol" when his hostess drove around the block to find a parking spot. A host of little experiences crowded in on the children: mosquitoes; screens on doors and windows; Hershey bars; the easy way people used telephones; being told to leave doors open after a lifetime of being told to shut them; slabs of butter so big that some children mistook them for cheese; the Mounties and, of course, the language. Travelers were quick to note that "People spoke decidedly different than in England." As one child wrote: "We say Toronto but here the people say Tronta. I first noticed that in Halifax when a man said 'You'll find Tronta a swell place'."

One little girl tried to sum up her first impressions in a letter home: "The story of when I arrived. Well I got off the boat and I thought I would have an awful time at the customs office but when I got there I mean at the customs office all the man asked us was what we had in our trunks and cases. I said clothes. Then we got into a bus it was very careless driving. We got out of the bus at a station we got on a train they look like GIANTS. We arrived at Toronto at half-past nine. Stephen was asleep and I had to wake him he got into a great temper. That night we slept in a place called Wymel-wood. In the morning we had to go out to a cafe. The next day I went 146 miles. I am going 600 in a few days."[7]

The children's arrival provoked a burst of emotion

that swept away Canadian reserve. People flocked to the docks at Montreal and Halifax to welcome them. At every stop along the line, a crowd would gather to hand the children candy, gum and apples. At the main terminals, crowds gathered to cheer the children and, at Saskatoon, three thousand people turned out at the station on August 24 to welcome twenty-five evacuees. The mayor himself was present in the biggest crowd seen in town since the King and Queen had stopped there the year before.

But the constant attention paid to the children began to worry immigration and railway officials, who became concerned for the children's safety, health and long-term adjustment. At many stations, the police did their best to hold back the crowds. Railway police were ordered to "prevent visitors from feeding the children confectionery" while maintaining public goodwill by collecting the candy and handing it to the escorts. Often the men simply handed it to the children. The escorts were instructed to "avoid small groups of children collecting around dogs and petting them" and to prevent people from asking the children about "the war, their homes and parents." Keeping children away from dogs and candy, however, was a hopeless task — as was preventing adults from asking questions. Among the most persistent questioners were newspapermen in search of human-interest stories. Newsreel cameras greeted the children and the National Film Board's John Grierson planned a documentary on the evacuation. (Some months later, his sister was lost at sea while travelling with a party of evacuees to film the crossing.) The newspapers were filled with photos and stories of the evacuees all through

July and August of 1940. The first photos were of private evacuees, with many references to flaxen hair, blue eyes and pink cheeks. As the CORB children arrived, the newspapers reported their lower social position, although the Montreal *Gazette* took care to assure its readers that the children "could hold their own ground with the privately sponsored children who had preceded them."[8]

From the start, seavacuation was clouded by the very real danger of an ocean crossing in wartime. Of the CORB children sent to Canada, more than four hundred children were on ships that were torpedoed. The first torpedoing occurred on the night of August 30 off the west coast of Ireland. The *Volendam*, carrying 321 CORB children among its passengers, was hit by a torpedo at 10 p.m. The children were quickly assembled at their lifeboat stations, and despite the darkness and confusion, safely put into the boats. The children sang as they were rowed away from the ship and were soon picked up by escorting vessels and returned to Glasgow. In a wave of publicity, 320 children returned to Glasgow. Mackenzie King said that the torpedoing "could not fail to fill the minds of all humane people with a sense of horror." Berlin replied that "the story smells . . . it is undoubtedly designed for American consumption." Shakespeare was convinced that his policy of escorted crossings had paid off and was happily photographed with the survivors. Most of the children were reported to be eager to go again and one thirteen-year-old boy from Newcastle argued, "It's a million to one chance of anyone being torpedoed, and I've had my chance. I won't be torpedoed again . . . please let me sail and go to

Canada before my mother knows. She's nervous and will try to stop me."

The celebratory mood was shattered when a final count showed that a boy was missing from the party. Shakespeare returned to London in despair at the loss. Shortly afterwards, however, he was hurrying back to Scotland. As it turned out, the *Volendam* had not sunk, but had been kept afloat by a small crew after the explosion. Robert, the missing boy, had been asleep when the ship was hit and had slept on as the passengers escaped. He woke at midnight to find himself alone in his cabin. When he went on deck the ship appeared to be deserted, so he decided to go back to bed. In the morning, he began to explore the vessel and was discovered by the crew as he collected pieces of the torpedo for a souvenir. Despite his protests that he wanted to stay on board, he was transferred from the *Volendam* to a destroyer and returned to Glasgow. Shakespeare met him there both to welcome him home and to swear him to secrecy.[9]

Little more than two weeks later, a second ship was torpedoed. This time, there was no happy ending. The *City of Benares* sailed from Liverpool on Friday, September 13, carrying ninety CORB children, including some *Volendam* survivors, and nine escorts among its complement of 408. For three days, the convoy sailed westward under naval escort until it was well beyond Ireland and in what were thought to be safe waters. The naval escorts turned back to more urgent duties, and the convoy sailed on in heavy seas six hundred miles off the Irish coast. At 10 p.m. a torpedo smashed into the ship's side. Some children were killed by the explosion, but the survivors were hurried on deck by the escorts, dragging on what clothes they could over their pajamas and nightdresses. The children crowded into the boats, but heavy seas swamped them as they hit the water, and the passengers were soon waist-deep in icy water as rain and hail began to fall. All about the boats, survivors clung to life rafts. Within half an hour of the explosion, the *City of Benares* listed and sank, carrying many of her passengers and crew down with her.

The survivors had no help from the other ships in the convoy, which had obeyed the standing order to scatter under attack. For eighteen hours they struggled to stay alive as they waited for rescue, but by the time the Royal Navy arrived many of the children had died of exposure. The first reports put the number of dead at 294 including eighty-three evacuee children. Eight days after the *City of Benares* went down, an RAF Sunderland on patrol spotted a lifeboat from the ship. Among the forty-six on the boat were six CORB boys who had been kept alive by the efforts of their escorts, Mary Cornish and Father O'Sullivan. Miss Cornish had massaged the boys, forced them to sing songs and kept up their spirits with an endless serial story of Bulldog Drummond. Shakespeare recommended Miss Cornish for the British Empire Medal. In all, seventy-three CORB children and six escorts died on the *City of Benares*. Among the victims were two survivors of the *Volendam* and five brothers and sisters from a single family.

The sinking stunned the public and marked the end of the CORB evacuation. As soon as news of the sinking reached London, Shakespeare ordered all the children ashore and six hundred CORB children were disembarked from ships about to sail. One of those ships was sunk twelve hours out of port. On October 3, 1940, the government announced an end to overseas evacuation for the winter. Nine parties totalling 1,532 children had reached Canada, 577 children went to Australia, 202 to New Zealand, 353 to South Africa and 828 to the United States under the sponsorship of a private committee. The U.S. Committee stopped sending children to the U.S.A. within a week of CORB's decision. The sinkings persuaded many parents to abandon plans of private evacuation, and Major Ney's schemes to resume school evacuations foundered on the growing reluctance of parents to risk their children to the Atlantic in winter.[10]

By February 1941, it had become plain that the evacuation would not resume. At a meeting of Canadian and British representatives in Ottawa that month, Keith Jopson said that there were still 14,000 children ready to go in Britain. That figure was significantly lower than the 24,000 approved in October and suggests Britain's loss of interest in the scheme following the tragedy. The provinces were still prepared to find homes for thousands of children but there, too, enthusiasm was waning among families faced with higher costs or the changed circumstances brought on by a father's enlistment. In 1941, only 458 children were privately evacuated to Canada, less than one-tenth the number of private evacuees in 1940. Weighing the risks, most parents preferred to keep their children at home. There would be no new demands for evacuation in the spring.[11]

CHAPTER IV

❖

THE
OTHER SHORE

❖

JOHN HUTTON: Age 7
CORB Evacuee

"At dusk the ship left the quayside, and the next morning all around the horizon we saw a great gathering of ships. We were sailing in convoy as protection against enemy submarines. We were protected against surface raiders by two great capital ships, thought to be the *Hood* and the *Renown,* which we could see on the horizon. Some years before, probably in 1937, I had been taken with a coach party, to visit the fleet at Chatham on a Navy Day. The presence of these two great ships therefore made an extra impression on my youthful imagination. We were at sea for two weeks; our time well spent with lifeboat drills and other activities organized by the directing staff who accompanied us to Canada. There was, too, at bedtime, the novelty of sleeping at close quarters in bunks.

"Eventually we disembarked in Halifax, Nova Scotia, laden with our suitcases and rucksacks and, after walking through what seemed to be an endless series of tunnels, found ourselves at a railway station. We were surprised to discover that Canadian railway platforms were very low and that we needed help to climb, luggage-laden, the steps into the Pullman carriages. The journey to Toronto, three nights and four days, seemed interminable, broken only by the excitement of eating meals in the dining cars and sleeping in bunks which unfolded from the ceiling. My chief recollection of the journey is of seemingly endless forests and lakes relieved by clusters of wooden buildings situated in small clearings. Later we came to more inhabited farmlands to cross the St. Lawrence, to catch a glimpse of Lake Ontario and finally on to Toronto. I recall coming out of the station, each with our luggage, a small crocodile of children, to be greeted by loud cheers from a party of adult Canadians. I had no idea what this cheering was about."

John went with the other children to the University of Toronto while the agencies prepared to place him with a family. A short time after his arrival, he was taken to live with a family in the city. His foster father was an immigrant from Yorkshire and his foster mother Canadian-born. They had one daughter, who was younger than John, and the family lived in an apartment over the family bakery. It was a big change from the large house in Colchester. The family made John welcome and took him on trips out of town to visit his foster mother's parents on their small farm.

Here, in the Indian summer, he ate his first corn on the cob, and on hot evenings, the family drove out to a beach on Lake Ontario for a swim.

Despite such efforts to please, however, John grew increasingly "withdrawn and secretive in some ways." Like many other guest children, he hid his stress behind fibs and minor misdemeanors and his foster mother, try as she might, could not break through his reserve. When the school year opened, John began classes at the Normal Modern School, riding there with his foster sister on the streetcar. Winter came, and with it the chores and pleasures of a Canadian boy's winter: "shovelling and sweeping the snow outside the shop, tobogganing and snowballing in the nearby parks and in the ravines."

John's foster father was a reservist and early in 1941 he was called to regular service. The bakery was shut, and John's foster mother and sister prepared to move away from Toronto. They decided not to take John with them, and the visitor from the Social Welfare department who had called on John every month now came more often to plan his move. Early in May 1941, Miss Chesnutt drove John to nearby Agincourt, "a pleasant village with maple tree-lined avenues." They stopped outside "a square two-storied house with a verandah, on the outskirts of the village," where John's new foster family, the Pelletts, were waiting. His foster father was an engineer and manager, his foster mother a housewife. They had two children, both younger than John—four-year-old Doris, and six-year-old Bobbie. "I made myself at home immediately. I had brought from England a large meccano set which was soon emptied onto the living-room carpet, much to the delight of the children. My new home was, from the beginning, exceptionally warm and hospitable." Mr. Pellett was descended from a Cornish family and Mrs. Pellett was the daughter of a Londoner. John's foster mother soon established a closeness with him that helped him cope with his "sense of deprivation" and his nervousness. Almost a year after his arrival in Canada, John had finally found his new home.

NINA LAVILLE: Age 11
CORB Evacuee

Nina's party travelled to Halifax on the *Anselm* in a convoy shadowed by submarines. "At some time during the first few days I remember being escorted one bright moonlight night onto the top deck attired in my warmest clothing topped by a life jacket. Even this evoked no great fear—just a sense of the dramatic—moonlit ships silhouetted against the skyline. Certainly the atmosphere was electric that night."

Safely in Halifax, Nina was put on the train for Regina. She was the only child in her party to be going that far west, and the passengers and crew took a great interest in the little English girl. As the train emerged from the bush, she encountered a new, and disturbing landscape: "I was just bewildered with the Prairies— all that space just sitting there doing nothing. . . . Mind you, I was disappointed to find neither Buffaloes nor Indians."

The train journey ended at Regina. Miss Phin, who was in charge of evacuees in Saskatchewan, met

Nina at the station and "drove me to my Uncle Mark's house, leaving two farm gates open [and] allowing a neighbor's horses to escape so everyone knew I had arrived. My Uncle Mark was working in the fields with a horse-drawn piece of machinery—I later found out it was called a binder. My small cousin took me to meet him. I jumped up on the back of the binder and was instantly at home on the farm that was to be home for five very happy years."

DAVID BROWN: Age 8
Rotary Evacuee

David remembers little of his trip on the *Duchess of Richmond*. He was seasick, of course, and "a sailor walked me around the deck to cure it." In better moments, he was intrigued by the gun that was mounted at the stern of the ship and even more fascinated by "the enormously large baths that used sea water." When the ship docked in Montreal, David and Jan were told to wait in the lounge until their names were called. The wait grew longer and longer, and as the last passengers went ashore the children became increasingly anxious.

On the dockside, David's foster parents were trying to cut "the usual red tape" and overcome the confusion in the sheds to reach the ship and collect the children. At last, David heard his name called, and he and Jan were introduced to the Luke family. Once the children's luggage had been collected, everyone packed into the family car for the drive home to Montreal's West End. The Lukes had three children, and their two teenage girls were at the dock to meet David and Jan. His ten-year-old foster brother, Morley, was away at camp. David was happy to explore the house and play with Morley's toys, and his foster family found the two British children "charming." The Lukes were of British origin and were Anglicans. Mr. Luke was an architect in his late thirties and the family lived "in a small home I built for myself in the lush year 1929." The family was athletic and outdoorsy and "all pretty bilingual." David and Jan soon felt at home.

Meanwhile, Jan's host family was vacationing on the Gaspé Peninsula, and the two children travelled there by train to spend August with them. The children beachcombed and built sandcastles. David caught fish, and the family picnicked off them on the beach. The children found themselves petted and fussed over by the guests at a nearby hotel. "Gifts, dolls, balls and lollipops and chocolates were daily affairs" their hostess wrote. "Indeed, we had to make a rule that they must not go to the Hotel." The Canadian children set to work to correct their guests' pronunciation and "check on any slips in Canadianisms." Jan's foster family was "a deeply religious one," and there were family prayers and bible readings every day: "David's prayer last night was 'God bless Mother and Daddy and keep them all safe in England, and keep us all safe in Canada.'" But the round of fun on the beach and the busy family life kept homesickness at bay. As the family was leaving Metis Beach to return to Montreal, David told his hostess that "he is planning to spend next summer with us at Metis. I said 'David dear, I trust next summer will see the war over and you and Janette safely back with your Mummy and Daddy.' He really hadn't thought of that. He says 'I shall have become very Canadian. I do like Canada' and he does."

MARY ANN WAGHORN: Age 7
CORB Evacuee

To Mary Ann, the *Duchess of York* seemed cramped and drab: "Children of all ages, many — probably most — sick. Our chaperone must have had a rough time, but I cannot recall her cheerfulness or patience once slipping. I cannot remember how the days were filled. One memory is of the frequent lifeboat drills, how cold it was. I am certain I recall the outline of other ships in the distance." On August 11, her parents received a cable to say the ship had docked safely.

Mary Ann stayed at Hart House while the Toronto Children's Aid attempted to match her to a family. Although her aunt took a great interest in Mary Ann, it was "utterly impossible" for her to give her niece a home. She was consulted, however, and had a long talk with a social worker "about the kind of home I thought Mary should go into." It all took time, and the little girl spent a few weeks in Hart House before she was sent to live with Coral and Roland Mann in Leaside, then a small town of four thousand on the outskirts of Toronto.

The Manns had close links with Britain, as Mr. Mann's parents had been born in England and his wife's family came from Scotland. It was this British tie that led them to volunteer to take in a guest child. Since they had a twelve-year-old boy of their own, they had suggested that a girl between six and eight would

69

best suit their family. "As a child I was told that they had always wanted a little girl of their own, had asked for a girl with blonde hair and blue eyes and having seen me (without my being aware of them) chose me. Only in later years did they tell me the obvious, that they felt it was one way in which they could make a positive contribution to the war effort. I count myself lucky to have fitted their 'order'."

Mr. Mann was a claims manager with an insurance company, and his wife had been a teacher before her marriage. Their family, like the Waghorns, had "an affectionate and welcoming array of aunts, uncles and cousins (I was the youngest by some years)." Mary Ann was glad to have a home again. The journey and the weeks at Hart House had been unsettling. She had watched many of her party "go quickly on their way directly to relations, whereas those awaiting foster homes as I was (but of course did not know) were in some kind of limbo." Worried at first about when she and her aunt would begin their "holiday," she was now "well pleased with my new home."

THE CURTIS FAMILY
CORB Evacuees

Five children travelling together, including a set of twins, was a natural subject for newspaper photographers, and the Curtises' photo appeared in several publications after the *Duchess of York* docked in Halifax. CORB had decided to send the family to Winnipeg, so the ocean crossing was followed by a long train ride. While Hazel and Fred marveled at "the vastness of everything and the wide-open spaces," Geoff could only wonder, "was the train ride never going to end?" The children were given a friendly welcome on the train and along the way, where they received "little parcels of food, drinks and sweets at every stopping station." But although many people made a special fuss over the Curtis brood on their journey, finding one home for all the children proved impossible. The tightly knit family would have to be broken up. Hazel found the days in the reception center "the worst part," as she watched her brothers and sister taken away. She felt responsible for the younger children, and she talked to the families that came to collect them. After they were settled, she wrote to her parents to tell them that all the children were in good homes. The youngest boys, Geoff and Tony, were the first to leave. Mrs. Ross, the head of the CAS in Winnipeg, called one day to see if there were two young girls she could take home. She was persuaded instead to take the twins. Fred and Muriel left together to live with a retired couple, and, finally, Hazel was invited to live with a couple who had a daughter her own age. Originally commissioned to look after the younger children, Hazel instead bore witness to her family's disintegration.

JOHN JARVIS: Age 5
CORB Evacuee

There were five hundred children on the *Duchess of York* and John stayed close to his brother, Michael, during the trip to Montreal and Toronto. In Toronto, the party settled into the reception center at the

University. By then, John was tired and ill, and he was put to bed by the staff.

The boys were placed with Mrs. Foster, who ran a peach farm outside Grimsby. She was an English immigrant who had a grown son serving in the RCAF. At this time, he "was home on leave most weekends" and took the boys under his wing. John "remembers him showing me 'a commando knife.' I was very impressed." Mrs. Foster herself was "so very kind to them" and her home was "happy and cheerful" and welcoming. John settled in quickly and felt secure with Mrs. Foster, who wrote to say that he "puts his arms around her neck and loves her." Mrs. Jarvis "missed the boys dreadfully, but when things begin to happen am so glad they went when they did." Each day, she looked for a letter from Grimsby.

BETTY HEELEY: Age 9
Rotary Evacuee

Betty's voyage on the *Duchess of Atholl* was a mixture of excitement and misery. Although the stewards and sailors were "extremely kind" to her, there was little they could do to ease her pain of separation and the overwhelming miseries of seasickness. Betty and her friend Brenda were both very seasick, and so was Betty's doll, Christine, but Paddy happily played nurse to them all. Brenda and Paddy's cabin mates helped the children when they could, but the four children spent most of their time helping each other and forming a close bond.

Once in Montreal, Betty was amazed at how large everything seemed in Canada. She was charmed by the lighted streets after nearly a year of blackout in Holmfirth. The children were taken for a meal "in a large room" and organized into parties for the journey to their new homes. The meals were served and the organizing done by "many ladies," and two of those ladies swooped down to tell Brenda and Paddy that new arrangements had been made for them to stay in Quebec with a Catholic family. Brenda and Paddy had no warning of this change in plans, and the children broke down and cried. "The younger girl was lying on the floor crying and screaming and was dragged away." Scared and "quite bereft" after her two friends disappeared, Betty clung to Michael when they were put on the train to travel on to Windsor, alone.

At 2:30 in the morning, the train pulled into Windsor station. Betty was half asleep, but when Michael jumped up and peered out of the window at the dark platform, she went over to stand by him. They could see a small party of adults and children on the platform looking anxiously at the train. Suddenly, one of the women in the party began jumping up and down on the spot. Michael turned to his sister and said, "I hope that's not mine!" After a quick welcome, Michael was driven away by his parents and their four children. The woman Michael had feared would be his foster mother turned out to be Betty's instead: "Edith could see my name on the label I was wearing on my coat." Bereft again after her brother's departure, Betty clutched her doll Christine close on the car journey to her new home.

Edith and Ross Hardy had heard of the evacuee

scheme through the Rotarian minister of their church. They had wanted children for years, and had even planned to adopt a child. The Hardys welcomed Betty with joy, and she attached herself to them immediately. In a day, she felt "secure and well loved" in her new family. For the first few days, her foster mother slept with her and made "a fuss" of her; Betty responded to her new Uncle and Auntie with a warmth that would make her a part of their family for the rest of their lives.

Betty soon found that the Hardy family was much like her own back in Yorkshire. Her foster mother had given up a job as a social worker after her marriage, and was now a full-time housewife. Her foster father worked as a stores supervisor and the family lived comfortably. Betty "had been used to a car in England" so it was no novelty in Canada, but she was delighted to find that Auntie, unlike her mother, could drive and was able to take her out shopping and visiting friends. She enjoyed the attention showered on her by Mrs. Hardy's friends, and her foster mother watched with amusement as Betty, swollen with importance, told her tales of the journey to sympathetic adults. After a while, she found the endlessly repeated questions irritating. Her father wrote to remind her that she "must be very patient and try to like answering the questions. Remember that you are a representative of England and you must give people a good impression of English children."

FRED: Age 13
CORB Evacuee

The novelty of life on board the R.M.S. *Anselm* took Fred's mind off his doubts about the separation from his family. He was also kept busy looking after his younger brother, who was seasick for the first couple of days. There were daily boat drills plus happier activities for the CORB party. Fred had "a part in the ship's concert" one night and he felt a thrill watching "the Royal Naval Ships in the escort and feel[ing] the tenseness of the situation. Then the relief as land came into view." The crossing brought them to Halifax, where the children boarded a train for their journey to Manitoba.

Fred found Canada exciting and was "impressed by the friendliness of the people—both of CORB and the numbers who turned out to see us at our various rail stops. I was amazed by the size of the trains on the CNR system." Fred took in the details with the eye of a boy who had grown up in a railway household, and he especially noticed "the level crossings, the bells and the train warning system. The vastness of the country and the change of scenery as we travelled from Halifax to Winnipeg—I think the journey took three days and two nights." From Winnipeg, the boys went to the village where their uncles lived. One was to stay with his uncle in the village, but Fred had been nominated to stay with his father's other brother, who had a farm and market garden outside the village.

The boys were not expected. Although Fred's father had nominated his two brothers to care for the children, the boy's uncles had not been told. Nor was

Fred's uncle happy to learn of his new responsibility. The Child Welfare people were not too happy, either, as neither of the homes had been inspected or approved. Incredibly, they decided to leave the boys with their relatives nonetheless.

The farm surprised Fred: "There were immense differences. Having been born and bred in a heavy industrial town in the north of England and moving to a farming community in the middle of Canada. There were no flush toilets and the whole of life was geared around the short productive season of the farm and garden. Life was so much hustle during the long summer days and there was no time to relax and see things. After the novelty of the first week or so had worn off, I didn't feel particularly welcome with my uncle." Fred was a long way from Yorkshire, and he was engulfed by a wave of desperate homesickness.

GRANIA O'BRIEN: Age 12
Lady Eden's School

Grania woke up one morning and found herself at sea. She was pleased and excited, even though the ship was "rolling fright[ful]ly." She spent the next two days in bed, reading and living on dry toast and honey; but on the third day, she began to enjoy the voyage. There were rumors that the convoy was being shadowed by U-boats and Grania sensed the tension among the adults, but for her it was "more of an adventure than anything to fear." The children discussed their chances of survival should the ship be torpedoed, and agreed that if they did have to jump into the sea, their heavy cork life jackets would probably knock them unconscious. They played games every day on deck, had long talks, read and ate the large meals with ice cream for "pudding" nearly every night. One memorable day, the *Duchess of Atholl* sailed past thirteen icebergs. After four days at sea, they saw Belle Isle and that night they had a party with Christmas crackers. The next day, there was a fancy-dress party. Grania and a friend dressed up as "England and Canada and we won a prize each — it was a pencil which had S.S. The Duchess of Atholl on." That night and the next they saw the Northern Lights.

Grania woke one morning and "knew something had happened." The *Duchess of Atholl* had docked in Montreal and men were already at work unloading the ship. The children were soon ashore and piling into taxis for the trip to the Windsor Hotel, where they spent the day before catching an evening train. Lady Eden was taking the school to Vernon, British Columbia, and the children were astonished as the days went by and Canada unfolded around them. Grania had expected the prairies to be sandy deserts; instead, they proved "very dull indeed, just long stretches of land." The Rockies, however, "were simply heavenly" and as the train crossed over the Great Divide, the children all crossed their fingers and made a wish. In Alberta, Grania saw "three cowboys and also some buffaloes." At every stop as the children walked along the station platform, people would come up to talk to them "and particularly commented on [the] red shoes we all wore." Most people gave the children sweets. At night, Grania lay in her "comfy" bunk and listened to the engine whistle's "lonely, haunting sound." She began to realize how far she was from home.

The journey ended with a long car ride to St. Michael's in Vernon. The children arrived at midnight on August 2, and it was morning before they had a good look at the building. St. Michael's had been a school, but it was in great disrepair by the time Grania's school arrived on the scene.

Lady Eden's school was one of the private schools that quickly ran into trouble. Grania knew nothing of the details, but she was soon aware that there was not enough money around to meet the costs. The school's sponsors helped, but Lady Eden decided she could not continue operating her school in Vernon. Quite suddenly, in February 1941, the children were told that they were moving. They travelled back across Canada to Breakeyville, a small town about fifteen miles outside Quebec. There Lady Eden reestablished the school in Chaudière House, which was lent to her by the Breakey family. Chaudière House would be Grania's home until she returned to England.

HAZEL WILSON: Age 14
CORB Evacuee

Hazel and her brother travelled to Halifax on the *Oronsay*, enjoying the ocean liner's comforts after the shortages of life at home. Once they arrived in Canada, Hazel's excitement grew: "I had just taken geography on Canada the previous year and couldn't wait to see Port Arthur and Fort William and the grain elevators." She was on her way to Winnipeg, rolling through "beautiful expanses of country just like the geography books," and sleeping every night in a berth. "One morning, we woke up on a siding in Winnipeg. We were taken to the School for the Deaf, where we were assigned dorms, sexes separated of course. From here, all our processing was done. One day, we were taken to the Children's Hospital, where we were really gone over physically." Hazel had not been nominated to anyone, and she could only wait as other children, including her brother, were matched with families.

Hazel tried to joke away her unhappiness: "At this school we were gradually picked up by assigned foster parents. A boy and I were the last to be taken as we were so old — fourteen — and really not cute. The poor boy finally went home with one of the volunteer house mothers. She was a lovely person. One day we were sitting forlornly on the front steps watching all the smart limousines coming to pick up kids, when we saw a couple (rather [an] odd couple we thought) *walking* up the long drive. We were a couple of nuts anyway, and I said 'These are mine — no car' and we laughed. Sure enough, soon my name was called and I went in. Bill Rook hugged me and asked if I liked music. I did really, so I said 'yes' and that was it, off we went — walking through City Park, and caught the bus at Deer Lodge to Woodhaven and home. I chatted all the way."

Hazel's foster father worked for John Deere, but his chief interest was music. Both he and his wife, Freda, were professional musicians active in the community and well-known to the childcare agencies. They had no children of their own and had volunteered to look after a guest child as part of their war work. To do so "they gave up things like season tickets to celebrity concerts and other expensive hobbies and personal enjoyments — like entertaining less." Hazel found it a sharp contrast with home. In Colchester she had little social life and few friends; most nights were spent at home and she felt shy and insecure in company. Her new family was outgoing and extroverted and Hazel found the sudden change "a bit overpowering" at first. It took time to adjust to life in the house on Woodhaven Boulevard, which would be her home until late in 1944.

CYNTHIA LORD: Age 11
St. Hilda's School

St. Hilda's was in for a rough crossing, and the convoy scattered in the heavy seas. The girls heard rumors of submarines and every night they went on deck for lifeboat drill. "We made friends with each other, too, but most of us were pretty sick and pleased when we were told our journey was over." The *Duchess of Atholl* docked in Montreal to a big welcome. Cynthia remembers "Mounties and people with gifts galore and press men and bands." She wrote home that "when we got off the ship we had our photos taken for the paper and cinema and when we were going to get on the train the people clapped and cheered and said 'Welcome to Canada'."

The school scattered while Sister Elsa, St. Hilda's Headmistress, searched for a building to house the 160 girls and their teachers. A number of the girls went to Cobourg, Ontario, and were housed in Hatfield House school. "For a while routine took over. . . . People turned up with clothes suitable for the summer days and we were inundated with invitations. We were even allowed into the cinema free." A local baker sent a cake with 'Welcome to Canada' on top. Sister Elsa was glad to accept offers to take the girls into private homes for the summer, and Cynthia and Helen went to stay with a childless couple in Cobourg, who would be their sponsors while they lived in Canada.

Cynthia enjoyed that summer: "The climate made the most difference. We had a beautiful beach, lots of swimming and were taken everywhere." She soon reported home that "I am getting a little bit brown." Cynthia called her sponsors Uncle and Aunt and found them more outgoing than her parents. In fact, "everyone was much more openly friendly. They weren't so academic as my family either." Although being with a family helped combat her homesickness, Cynthia's letters home reflected her anxiety about her parents and the danger from the blitz. Her parents had a shelter nicknamed "the Cyclone Cellar" — Cynthia was a Wizard of Oz fan — and in most of her letters home, Cynthia asked if there had been raids and if they had been using the cellar recently. "I do hope you are well and haven't been bothered by Jerry." "I do hope you are very well and haven't had any more visits to Cyclone cellar." Despite the sun, the swimming, the picnics, trips to Niagara and the Canadian Exhibition in Toronto, Cynthia could not always mask the tension of those days. Helen suffered the most from her moods and the two friends squabbled. Cynthia confided in a letter home: "Dear Mummie: Here is an extra bit to my letter. I don't think I can be friends with Helen because she is always wanting . . . to quarrel with me, and I said to her, 'You are very silly annoying me and trying to get me [in] a worse temper than David (which

81

she really does) because the next thing you will know is! — I *won't* be sticking up for you in school time if the girls are nasty to you.' Do you think I was right? Helen has been saying Red House is a much better school than St. Hilda's and she is absolutely horrid about it, and I just can't stand for it so Helen is perhaps crossed off the list. Yesterday went to ride Ann's pony and I can canter properly and Helen darnt. We also went out to [a] nice lake. Well, lots of Love, Cynthia." At times, her loneliness broke through as well: "I wish I was at home. If you come out to Canada, I will *have* to come home with you. You must promise me that I can come home in 6 months whether the war is over or not. If you don't I will swim. Please write to me every week."

By mid September, Sister Elsa had made her arrangements for the school. "We were all collected together in September and told one by one where we were going. The school was split up into several parts. It was awful standing in a big hall while a teacher read out names from a list. As we had only joined to go to Canada, we hardly knew anyone, and twenty of us were sent to Alma." Alma College was a private school in St. Thomas, Ontario. Cynthia described her new school in a letter to her family: "We are now at Alma College which is a girl's school about 100 miles away from Cobourg. Alma College is a very, very expensive school. The girls seem to look older than they are but I have quite a lot of friends now at Alma College. The school has a swimming pool and a gym. I will work hard and try to be good. It is really hard for me to be good and to work hard as I am not really used to it." Within a few days, Cynthia was sure that she would be happy at Alma.

CHAPTER V

❖

AN UNCERTAIN ADVENTURE

❖

THE whole thing is, as we all knew from the start an uncertain adventure. Perhaps it will turn out better than many expect."[1]

E.H. Blois

Until the 1920s, thousands of children were sent to Canada each year by British organizations, and the home boys and girls were a familiar sight in Canadian homes and on Canadian farms. The juvenile immigration had given some children fresh opportunity, but others suffered hardship, neglect and brutality. By 1940, all provinces except Saskatchewan and British Columbia had reacted to public pressure by passing laws to bar child immigrants. An Order-in-Council allowed the evacuees into Canada in 1940, but everyone involved wanted to be sure that this new juvenile immigration program would avoid the abuses of earlier days. As soon as the question of child refugees came up, F.C. Blair had turned to Charlotte Whitton, the Executive Director of the Canadian Welfare Council (CWC), who was well known for her concern with childcare. In some ways, Blair and Whitton were kindred spirits. Whitton shared Blair's prejudices and agreed with him that the CNCR was planning a large-scale movement of refugees to Canada. She, too, felt that if the refugees were "almost all . . . of either Catholic or Jewish religion" they would create intolerable pressure . . . to bring their families." After the decision was made to admit one hundred refugees, however, the CWC set up a Committee on Child Refugees to advise the CNCR, and it was closely involved in all the discussions on evacuees and refugees over the next few months.[2]

Whitton, unlike Blair, was neither circumspect nor skilled in the bureaucratic dance. She preferred the frontal assault and sharp denunciation of her opponents. Whitton was short-tempered and not too interested in the dull grind of routine administration. Dr. Fred MacKinnon, from Nova Scotia, who watched her at work during the planning for the evacuees in 1940, recalled that she was "a brilliant woman . . . but, alas, when it came to constructive and detailed planning, she preferred to baffle the participants with an endless flow of words." Among those who had felt the sharp edge of Whitton's tongue in earlier days were the agencies involved in juvenile immigration. In fact, her attacks had helped to bring child immigration to an end. Whitton had two intertwined concerns in her crusade. She wanted both to improve childcare by substituting foster homes for institutions and to develop a body of professional childcare workers in Canada. Only professional workers, she argued, would have the skill to select the proper home for a given child, supervise the placement to avoid the disasters that had marked juvenile immigration and produce happy and healthy citizens.[3]

The surge of concern for refugees threatened the gains Whitton had made in the past twenty years. She worried about the impact thousands of overseas children would have on the existing childcare agencies, and she was troubled by the sudden interest in the question of groups she regarded as non-professional. Whitton resented the fact that the National Council of Women called for easier entry into Canada for the children "contrary to . . . the considered opinion of the public and voluntary agencies actually in the field." As more and more private groups began to invite children to Canada, Whitton grew increasingly upset and spoke of trying "to stabilize the situation" by persuading them to work through established agencies. She knew that it took more than a spontaneous burst of goodwill to provide long-term care for children. There was a chance that evacuation would produce a crop of horror stories like the home-child schemes she had helped to end. If the children did come, Whitton wanted them cared for in ways that would advance her work, not undermine and destroy it.[4]

In February 1940, Whitton called a conference of provincial childcare agencies to plan for the one hundred CNCR-sponsored refugees. The delegates who met in Toronto assumed that, now the war had begun, the children might be the first of thousands. They agreed that it was vitally important to follow professional standards in choosing the children and placing them in homes. Many of the children, they knew, would be emotionally scarred and difficult to handle. Isobel Harvey, the Superintendent of Neglected Children in British Columbia, suggested that a psychological test in Europe should be part of the selection process. Most of the delegates agreed that this was desirable but difficult to arrange, and all agreed that while they were in "intense sympathy" with the children, only a conservative approach would "assure the children of a reasonably happy and successful absorption into Canadian life."[5]

The hundred refugees never did arrive, but by early summer the government had made its offer to take in at least 10,000 children. The Immigration Branch called two conferences of childcare experts on June 3-4 and on July 8 to plan the guest children's reception. At the first conference Immigration responded to British requests by asking the provinces what kind of children they preferred. The answers were quite specific. British Columbia wanted a mix of 88% Protestant, 10% Roman Catholic and 2% Jewish, which roughly corresponded to the homes available. Alberta preferred Protestant and British children. Toronto offered to take a "large number" of Jewish children, Montreal suggested a mix of 65% Roman Catholic, 25% Protestant and 10% Jewish. The Jewish agencies of Montreal, however, said they could arrange private home care for "as many Jewish children as it was deemed possible to bring out to Canada." Religion was not the only consideration in choosing children. Both Saskatchewan and Prince Edward Island wanted older children useful on the farm.

Whitton protested that Saskatchewan and Prince Edward Island were missing the point. This was not to be a revival of the home-children schemes, but an invitation to children to come to free homes as guests of Canadian families. No child should be placed in a home where the parents were on relief or where the child was invited for "money value." The delegates agreed that they were making a "patriotic contribution to the war effort" and that the children must be placed in homes as like their own as possible and without being expected to work for their keep. In July, the extent of the patriotic contribution began to worry some delegates. CORB was at work and the private evacuees were arriving in increasing numbers. T.A. Crerar did little to reassure them. Swept up in a tide of patriotism, he told the delegates that 15,000 homes had already been offered and that as many as 300,000 children might come to Canada from Britain. Not surprisingly, the provincial delegates found the Minister's speech disturbing. Ten thousand children would put a considerable strain on existing resources, but the prospect of 300,000 was terrifying.[6]

Dr. George Davidson, Director of Social Welfare in British Columbia, was seconded to the Immigration Branch to organize the evacuee scheme. This was not good news for Whitton, who had alienated many western agencies by giving them a clear impression that she believed eastern Canadians alone were fully professional. Whitton wanted to keep the coordination of the guest-child program in the hands of the CWC, but the practical problems of negotiating with the provinces and overseeing the evacuation were instead handled by the Immigration Branch and a National

Advisory Committee set up in August by the Dominion Government. Dr. R.C. Wallace, Principal of Queen's University, chaired the committee and Davidson became its technical expert. He and Blair worked with the British representative of CORB in Ottawa. Whitton at the CWC played a less prominent role in the evacuation as the administration grew more complex.[7]

After the July meeting, the provinces wanted to know what obligations they were accepting. It was Davidson who had the job of persuading them to sign an agreement with the Dominion government covering the CORB children. Under the agreement, Ottawa transported the children from the port to the province, paid for the extra staff hired to care for the evacuees and met the costs of any of the children if free care failed. The provinces assumed responsibility for the children, chose and inspected the homes and placed the children with approved families who agreed to provide care at their own expense. This apparently straightforward agreement took months to negotiate in the face of provincial suspicion. A.T. Proctor, the Minister of Highways in Saskatchewan, was also responsible for neglected children, and he was very cautious. He had run into trouble with Ottawa under an earlier agreement to share the costs of highway construction. Manitoba had been denied some unemployment relief by Ottawa. Davidson had to agree that the provinces had "a good deal of reason to be wary," and it was not until March 1941 that the agreement was signed.[8]

The guardianship question had to be thrashed out between provincial capitals, Ottawa and London. All the host governments wanted to know who would be legally responsible for a CORB child who needed an emergency operation or who was orphaned by the war. Shakespeare found the question a difficult one because it affected the rights of parents and governments, and he hoped it would go away if he ignored it. It did not. The British parents saw a transfer of guardianship as an invasion of their rights. The provinces regarded federal legislation as an invasion of their rights, and some began to act as the children's guardians. Ontario, to the distress of CORB, authorized operations on children without the knowledge of CORB or the parents. The British did not want to see the provinces made guardians of the children, but when London suggested that the foster parents assume the role, Jopson replied that the provinces would "shriek" if they lost this responsibility. The British, arguing that the parents would prefer a guardian "directly linked to this country," proposed an Act at Westminster making the British High Commissioner in Ottawa guardian. Phyllis Snow, who replaced Jopson in the spring of 1941, reported that this proposal had brought "a howl" from the provinces, which were "intensely jealous of their rights and privileges and react immediately against anything which might seem to impinge upon them." The shrieking and howling were stilled by a provision in the British Act of Parliament in May 1941, allowing the British High Commissioner to transfer guardianship to the provinces. Parents' rights were protected by allowing them to revoke the guardianship if they could convince the British government that they had made satisfactory alternative arrangements. Privately evacuated children remained the responsibility of their foster parents. At first, when private arrangements broke down, the British government transferred the children to the guardianship of the British High Commissioner, but in 1942 the provincial governments began to treat those children in the same way as they did Canadian children needing care. Blair agreed to "see how it works."[9]

The children arrived while these negotiations went on and the bills were paid by the Advisory Committee out of funds voted by Parliament. Whatever their suspicions of Ottawa, the provinces were eager to see the children well settled and making a good start in their new homes. It was no easy job. Despite the conferences and the talk of professional standards, childcare in Canada in 1940 was a haphazard affair. Many provinces lacked the organizations and the staff for supervised foster care. In most provinces, the Children's Aid Society (CAS) took responsibility for the work. A CAS was formed by a group of citizens who applied to their provincial government for recognition as the childcare agency in their community. The CAS were largely voluntary organizations that ran shelters for children and employed a small professional staff. They were generally found in towns and cities, but rarely in rural communities. The work of the CAS was supervised by provincial government departments that also took responsibility for neglected children where no CAS had been established. New Brunswick had no childcare services in 1940. Jopson reported that the province was "indebted to CORB for the impetus that has created a child welfare service throughout the Province" as a newly appointed Supervisor of Child Evacuees set up CAS in every county.

Some provinces had well-established and competently run departments caring for children although even the best lacked the staff they needed. British Columbia, Ontario and Manitoba were thought to be the leaders in this work. It was in British Columbia that Dr. George Davidson had made the reputation that preceded him to Ottawa. Isobel Harvey, the B.C. Superintendent of the Department of Neglected Children, ran a department that was said to have achieved the highest standards of childcare in Canada. In Ontario, B.W. Heise headed the Children's Aid Branch of the Department of Public Welfare. In Manitoba, Dr. J.W. Jackson ran the Department of Health and Public Welfare where the Child Welfare Division was in the charge of "capable and kindly Mrs. Sanders" and had a number of social workers to help supervise children in care. Alberta did not meet CWC standards. Neither Calgary nor Edmonton had a CAS in 1940, and Whitton had been critical of Alberta for years before the war after a CWC survey of the welfare agencies in Edmonton and Calgary found them inadequate. The Department of Child Welfare and T.R. Blaine, the Superintendent of Neglected Children, both aroused Whitton's wrath. When Blaine announced, in June 1940, that he had no place for "scientific child welfare," he alienated many members of Edmonton's Refugee Committee. The feud between Whitton and Alberta became public late in 1940, when her criticisms of the way Alberta handled the guest children were published. Whitton won the argument and the only CORB children sent to Alberta were those nominated to join families in the province. Marjorie Maxse was more sympathetic to Alberta. In 1944, she reported that the lack of scientific care by trained workers "does not appear to have had any ill effects on CORB children."

Childcare in Saskatchewan was little better than in Alberta. There were CAS in the four largest towns and a Bureau of Child Protection in the Department of Highways. The CAS in Saskatoon, however, was so poorly run that Whitton said it could not be used "under its present staff, for the set up we need in the emergencies of war time." Whitton suggested, confidentially, to the people in Saskatoon working with the CNCR that they set up a committee to bypass the CAS. The committee in Saskatoon worked well and was praised by Jopson for the "meticulous care" it took in placing the children. Outside the cities, however, it was difficult to create organizations that met the highest standards. Early in July 1940, A.T. Proctor called a meeting of delegates from municipalities, voluntary organizations and professional bodies to discuss the evacuee scheme. They agreed to set up local committees to "act as a culling committee . . . [to] eliminate those homes that don't appear to them suitable or satisfactory" on the basis of local knowledge. The children placed in approved homes would be supervised by the local clergyman. It was all rather far removed from Whitton's vision of professional childcare.

The Bureau of Child Protection in Regina came no closer to the ideal. T.A. Proctor appointed Ruby E. Gleiser as Director of Evacuee Children. She held the post until overwork brought on a heart attack in April 1941, and Anne P. Phin succeeded her. Ruby Gleiser impressed Davidson when he first met her as "a very capable and willing person," but over the years the situation in Saskatchewan worried CORB. Neither Gleiser nor Phin ever achieved a level of record keeping that satisfied CORB, and both women came to be regarded by childcare professionals as political appointees of a government permeated by jobbery. Gleiser was described by Maxse as an "amateur friend of the Minister" whose zeal outran her knowledge and Phin as "another political friend of the Minister . . . with neither knowledge nor judgment." Without professional skills and working alone to supervise children scattered all over the province, the two directors barely avoided serious disasters, in CORB's opinion. No records survive to indicate what particularly troubled CORB, but it was not surprising that CORB considered the level of supervision inadequate. Shortly after the socialist CCF government was elected in 1944, Phin was "advised to seek employment elsewhere" as a political appointee of Proctor's. She immediately resigned. "I would rather be a friend of a gentleman like I know Mr. Proctor to be—than work for any CCF government" she told a friend. Care of the evacuees was absorbed into the newly created department of Health and Welfare.[10]

Problems on the prairies could be bypassed by sending the children elsewhere, but shortcomings in Nova Scotia and Quebec were not so easily avoided. The children entered Canada through Halifax and Montreal. The agencies there would be called on to handle a heavy load. In Nova Scotia, Ernest H. Blois, a crusty and opinionated bureaucrat, had been Director of Child Welfare under one title or another since 1912. In 1939, Blois appointed Dr. Fred

MacKinnon, a newly graduated social worker, as his Assistant Director of Child Welfare. MacKinnon found that the province had neglected child welfare services for many years. The CAS were "poorly financed, understaffed and struggling against heavy odds to provide a minimal service." Two of the five professional social workers in the province were employed by the Department, but it was almost impossible to supervise children after they had been placed. MacKinnon went to work to improve the services in the province in the face of the expected demand. In Quebec, there were no CAS and Dr. Jean Gregoire, Deputy Minister of Health, supervised a confusion of childcare agencies affiliated, for the most part, with religious organizations. Thousands of private evacuees, some of whom needed help, were pouring through Montreal as the discussions over CORB continued. In June 1940, the CNCR and the Child Refugee Committee of the Montreal Council of Social Agencies met and organized the Council for Overseas Children (COS). Gregoire accepted it as the agency to handle evacuees and refugees in Montreal and towns as far away as Trois Rivières. The COS was chaired by William Birks, Chairman of CNCR in Montreal, and it set up an operating committee under Dr. Grant Fleming, a former dean of medicine at McGill University. Fleming was a hard-working and sympathetic man, but he was new to the business of providing care for children.[11]

In many communities, volunteer committees helped the agencies find homes for the CORB children and care for the private evacuees who ran into difficulties. In the early summer, those caring for the children stopped calling them evacuees and began to use the more welcoming label of guest children or guests. When CORB was announced, thousands of families offered to take in a guest. In Vancouver the Child Welfare Bureau was swamped with callers, and the staff did no regular work for weeks as they coped with the offers. The Bureau had to ask for volunteers to help with registration. In the first days of the response, child placement workers began to worry that many volunteers were responding to a wave of enthusiasm without thinking far enough ahead. People remember offering to take in a child "to help the war effort," or because "it was the humane and patriotic thing to do," or because "they felt sorry for them and decided if they could keep one child safe from the bombings it would be wonderful." Betti Sandiford, at the University of Toronto, reminded her committee that "the scheme was entered into to help Britain in time of dire peril and distress and not to provide people with ready-made and charming families." Taking in a child meant taking on obligations that could not be "lightly overthrown because they may interfere with our comfort."

The National Council of Women had registered 100,000 homes in September 1939, and the start of the evacuation brought in more offers. The offers came from people at all levels of Canadian society. In Nova Scotia, MacKinnon found most offers came from the "middle class or at least middle income" families. In Ontario, the first homes offered and approved by the end of August were ranked by occupation of head of household. The biggest group were working men, skilled, semiskilled and laborers. Then came professionals, including teachers and clergymen, followed by farm homes. In Saskatchewan, Proctor found that "it is the people in the financial group least able to bear the extra expense that have taken these children" and many had to be helped financially.[12]

CAS workers and public health nurses were given the job of assessing the homes, and they worked at great speed in the summer of 1940. By July 30, for example, Ontario had approved 5,000 homes and by March 1941, 12,823 homes had been inspected and 7,035 approved. British Columbia approved 1,201 of 1,388 homes offered and Manitoba approved 2,216 homes. The inspector usually made one visit to the home and assessed it and the family. She rejected homes that were too small or badly kept. Volunteers who were thought to be too old or were ill or living alone were told that they could not take in a child. Some families with incomes as low as $600 were approved, but poverty or the hope of making money by foster care were reason enough to reject a home. The inspections disposed of many of the homes offered to the National Council of Women because the families were on relief or required subsidies to take in the children. This rapid inspection of the home and assessment of the family was the base on which the match of home and child was made.[13]

The key to the professional child placement preached by Whitton was a careful match of child and home. The first priority was a religious one. All children were to be placed in homes of their own denomination. Davidson assured Bishop Harold Sexton that "we would be governed almost exclusively by the matter of religion." There were, however, only three religious categories used — Protestant, Catholic and Jew — which distressed those Anglicans like Sexton who did not regard themselves as members of "a Protestant sect." Social workers were flexible on this question. When there were complaints from neighbors that some foster parents were not attending church in Winnipeg, Mrs. Sanders merely noted that "if all children were withdrawn from homes where parents do not attend church although the children do, there would be a great many replacements to be made." Saskatchewan had anticipated that problem when its agreement with foster parents required them only "to send the said child . . . to the religious services" of his church.

It was easy enough to match the child with a family of the same denomination, but a social match was harder to make. Both CORB and Canadian governments assumed it was best "to try to keep the children in the same general strata they came from." This was the unspoken principle behind many of the private evacuation schemes matching the children of British and Canadian professionals. The CORB children, however, were not easy to evaluate. All the host countries complained of the lack of information among the papers the children carried. Canadian authorities vainly tried to match hundreds of undersized, poorly clothed and excited children, speaking in a wide range of accents, to equivalent Canadian homes. A few questions about their parents' occupations gave a clue, but most guest children found themselves living at a higher standard than they had known at home — even when they were as closely matched as possible. A working-class home in Canada could seem luxurious to a working-class child from Glasgow.

It was difficult to find homes for large families. Ontario claimed to have 15,000 places available in 5,000 homes by the end of July 1940 but the figure was impossibly optimistic. Most foster parents had children living at home and could take in only one or two guest children. The foster families also had preferences that had to be considered. There was no difficulty finding homes for little girls, but many volunteers were unsure about taking in teenagers. Teenaged boys were the hardest to place, and Maxse felt that "the arrival of sturdy adolescents who looked more suitable for the recruiting officer than a foster home" made a bad impression in Canada. Ten percent of the CORB evacuees were over thirteen in the summer of 1940, and the provinces asked that younger children should come if the evacuation began again in 1941. Faced with problems of limited space and reluctance to take teenagers, the placement workers were often forced to split families. When it came to placing a teenager, any approved home would do if it meant rescuing a child from sitting in the reception center watching all the younger children leave for their new homes. The claims for scientific placement gave way before the practical considerations of finding a home for every child. The results were not always happy. Isobel Harvey acknowledged that "we certainly made some bad placements."

Many of the older guest children had been registered for evacuation by their parents so that they could look after the younger children in the family. That link was broken by the separate placements. In some cases, experience suggested that it would be better to separate children who had been found homes together. Older children were sometimes bossy or domineering toward their younger brothers and sisters or were thought to be encouraging them to be cheeky and uncooperative toward their foster parents. In a few homes, the guest children fought bitterly among themselves, and it was impossible to know if this was their usual behavior at home or a consequence of the tension of the first months in Canada. Foster parents faced with endless bickering and occasional violence between their guest children asked for them to be separated and the childcare authorities usually agreed to do so. Two brothers in British Columbia, for example, were separated because the older one was "mean [to] his nice friendly" younger brother and was making him unhappy by making him feel inferior. The younger boy was beginning to ape his elder brother and separation was thought to be beneficial for both boys.

CORB had agreed to attempt to send children to nominated homes and even to give priority to nominated children. But the system was cumbersome and caused many problems in the summer of 1940. Blair was annoyed when he had to hire a matron to travel with three nominated children from the first CORB party who were the only ones going to British Columbia. Some parents were tempted to make nominations to distant relatives and casual acquaintances just to get their children on the boat. Jopson wrote of "children producing from the pockets at the last moment scraps of paper on which their parents had written the names of old friends and acquaintances." In one case a child was nominated to a family met years before at a cocktail party.[14]

The nominated homes had to be approved before the children were placed and that made extra work. Some agencies were unwilling to turn down a nominated home even if it seemed to be unsuitable. Ruby Gleiser had doubts about some of the homes in Saskatchewan, but rather than interfere with the nominations, she decided to wait until "the enthusiasm wears off" before suggesting a move. T.R. Blaine, in Alberta, was less diplomatic and refused to place a child "from a family of good home" with a family he thought unsuitable. The result was "quite a furor in the town where these people reside and are apparently well thought of." In Montreal, the COS held children in the reception center for as long as a month while they tried to find out something about the nominated family. In rural provinces and in less accessible parts of Quebec, it was difficult to arrange supervision of the widely scattered children. Most professionals agreed that nomination was expensive and ineffective. They had another fear, too, as E.H. Blois perhaps unwittingly acknowledged when he commented on the fact that children were being placed in nominated homes or in homes chosen because the parents and foster parents were in the same line of work. If these placements work, he said, "then some of us will have to revise our conceptions of child placing." Many of them did work but enough failed under the weight of what Maxse called "resentful obligation" to convince childcare workers that their skills improved on chance or the ties of family and friendship.[15]

In most provinces, the children stayed in reception centers while they recovered from the voyage and were medically examined and interviewed by the placement workers. Hart House at the University of Toronto housed seven hundred children during the summer and other buildings up and down St. George Street were pressed into service. Residential schools empty in the summer holidays were used as reception homes from Halifax to Saskatoon, but in some towns private houses were lent or rented. Only in Alberta was no effort made to house the children when they arrived. The centers were equipped with donations of furniture and linen from public institutions, and the small paid staff were helped by volunteers chosen from among teachers and others who worked with children. The centers were supplied with games and painting rooms, swings in the gardens and books in the libraries. They were staffed with men and women eager to welcome the children, but they could be lonely places nonetheless — especially for the children who were the last of their party to find a home.

All the children had been medically examined a couple of times before they left Britain, and they were examined again in the centers to ensure that they met provincial health requirements. Canadian doctors found the guest children undersized, underweight and under-protected. Most provinces required children to be vaccinated against smallpox, inoculated against diphtheria and to be tested for tuberculosis. "We do not feel we should take a chance on the children spreading . . . diseases among the people," one provincial minister explained. Some British parents objected to the vaccinations and inoculations but Canadian doctors were unsympathetic. G.F. Amyot, Provincial Health Officer of Ontario, said that Britain was behind the times and it was "appalling" that "ignorance . . . should be permitted to interfere with the procedure that is accepted scientifically" for the protection of children. If the children did not carry with them a sworn statement from their parents objecting to inoculation, they received the injections.

The disease that most worried Canadian authorities was tuberculosis. Health standards had improved enough in Britain in the years before 1940 that the rate of those unfit to serve in the war was half what it had been in 1914. Deaths from tuberculosis had dropped dramatically, but 27,000 people died of the disease in 1940 and the incidence remained high. Public health authorities in Canada had campaigned against tuberculosis since the early days of the century, and Dr. Davidson was alarmed by an article in a British medical journal that urged doctors to send tubercular children to Canada. The Canadian medical officer in England, H.B. Jeffs, rejected children from homes where there was active TB, but he accepted those from homes where there had been an active case as recently as three years ago. Because of the concerns of public health doctors, all the children were tested for TB and many showed positive reactions. Half the CORB children in Manitoba tested positive. Even the middle-class children of British university faculty evacuated to Toronto showed "quite a few positive reactions." Subsequent x-rays happily showed no active cases in either group, but a few children with TB entered Canada in other parties of children. Ironically, the only CORB child who died of TB contracted the disease in Canada.

Jeffs reviewed 26,864 medical certificates in the summer of 1940 and rejected slightly more than 8%

of the children, mostly because of physical defects and mental deficiency. The number of rejections would have been much higher if Jeffs had turned away children with bad teeth. Jeffs not only passed these children, but even stopped asking that they be treated before going to Canada. He was upset because British dentists usually extracted children's teeth, and Jeffs hoped that they would get better treatment in Canada. F.C. Blair was outraged by Jeffs' policy. "We did not bring these children to Canada to supply dental care which they had not had overseas," he told Heise. "The condition of their teeth was not a matter that the Dominion Government could undertake to correct." The children came anyway and presented the authorities with a major problem in the first months of their stay.[16]

Once the children had been given a clean bill of health and had been interviewed to assess their background and personality, they were placed in an approved home. The guest children had little say in where they were placed. Some of them asked for a home in a rural community or near a friend made on the voyage. The requests were difficult to meet, especially if one of the children was nominated. Some children were able to influence their choice of home. Jean, a strong-willed eleven-year-old, frustrated an effort to place her and her brother in a house where "she did not like the smell." The children sat on the stairs for hours, refusing to move, until they were returned to the children's shelter and found a new home.

A five-year-old boy was sent to stay with a friend at Christmas 1940 and liked the home so much that he stayed there until March 1941. When the childcare authorities found out what he had done, they agreed to let him stay in the home he had chosen for himself.[17]

Some children spent the war on Canadian farms. Most of them were nominated, but in Manitoba and some other provinces childcare agencies overcame their concerns about the problems of supervision and placed children with farm families. Adam, son of a Glasgow fireman, and his friend, Duncan, were two city boys who found themselves on farms in Manitoba where "everything was different." Molly Hyndman recalls the day when Adam and Duncan arrived. The Hyndmans had volunteered to take a girl but the district nurse phoned from Brandon one afternoon to ask if the Hyndmans would take in two boys who had become friends after leaving Scotland. Within minutes, Mrs. Hyndman had agreed to take Duncan and arranged for Adam to stay with her sister-in-law on a farm three miles away. The nurse brought the boys to the farm that same afternoon. Duncan and Adam were instantly swept into the routine of the farm, clambering into an old Chevy to take the afternoon lunch to the men in the fields. When Molly gave Duncan a cupful of milk, "he looked at me with big blue eyes and said 'Is *all* this for me?'" Then the boys rode off on the tractors with their foster fathers "not conscious of the unusual picture they made, so unmistakably British in this Canadian farm scene." Later, they discovered the evening chores of "milking, feeding chickens and gathering eggs, carrying water to the ponies and swill to the pigs" and separating the milk before feeding the skim to the calves. It was the beginning of a connection between the boys and their foster families that endures to this day. When rural placements worked well, the children were happy and adjusted easily to the great contrast between industrial England and rural Canada in 1940, where electricity was still uncommon and indoor plumbing unknown.[18]

Guest children who went to the city also found life very different from the one they had left behind. Many of them spent the first weeks with their new families in cottages by a lake or at the seashore. The days at the beach were a delight to the children and helped them to get to know their new families. The CORB children, in particular, tended to find the contrasts with home striking. Phyllis, a thirteen-year-old daughter of a factory worker in England, found herself living in "a very comfortable and spacious residence" with her own room. The family had a number of cars and owned a summer home at the lake. A thirteen-year-old boy happily settled into a home where the family had two cars and were well fed and comfortably clothed. The security of his new life was in sharp contrast to life in England and "what seemed like a continual fight for survival back home. We were poor!!" Canadian homes less luxurious than these still made a contrast to home. Nine-year-old Joyce and her sister went to live with a music professor in a home where money was sometimes tight. She was struck by the size of the house and the fact that the family owned a piano. The girls spent their first month at the beach with their hosts. "In England we were fortunate to get day trips to the seaside."

Some children of professional families had lived comfortably in Britain before their evacuation. For them, the contrast with home was still noticeable, although not so great. A thirteen-year-old girl, leaving her doctor father's home to stay with a Canadian doctor's family in Toronto, thought "they *seemed* rich . . . the whole cottage and camp thing was a new world." A nine-year-old girl thought that "money seemed easier" in her new home. What struck these children most in their first days was the greater ease that existed between servants and masters in Canada. The young girl thought "the Canadian housekeeper seemed much more of an equal in the household than did our resident maid in England." Nine-year-old Patricia also noticed "the ease with which the woman who came to clean the house sat down for a cup of tea with the mistress of the house. I remember thinking then—this is why the cleaner (who came from Glasgow) came to live in Canada—she is treated as an equal here." Eleven-year-old Mike also enjoyed the more relaxed Canadian ways. "We ate in the U.K. in a dining room with a cook and a maid. The cook was not very good. In Canada we ate in the kitchen—home cooking marvelous."

There was a lot for the children to learn about Canadian customs in their new homes but the evacuation to Canada did not produce the spectacular cultural clashes that had marked the earlier evacuations inside Britain. Few English children arrived in Canada dirty or with lice. Stories of children defecating in the drawing room or settling down to sleep under a bed, rather than in it, which were the commonplaces of English evacuee stories, were seldom heard in Canada. The abrupt end to the evacuation also meant that nowhere were there enough evacuees to dominate a community and form a separate group as they did in many English villages in 1940. Instead, the guest children joined their Canadian communities.[19]

One problem the guest children did face was the blaze of publicity and the glare of public attention that brought people flocking to the railway stations along their route. They were greeted with friendly curiosity in the summer of 1940 and were often showered with presents as they settled into their new homes. The gift-giving lasted at least until Christmas, 1940. At that time, school children gave presents to the guest children in their schools, and in one British Columbia community, "the loggers and fishermen of the district clubbed together to present an eleven-year-old child with a diamond bracelet."

Canadians who crowded around the children wanted to know about the war. The older children were asked to speak to clubs and schools, and all the children were cross-examined about their experiences in the blitz and on the journey to Canada. The warmth of these receptions could be upsetting. One boy of six taking part in a school concert was overwhelmed by the applause that greeted the announcement that he was a guest child. He "was so confused that he forgot his part, much to his chagrin and that of his foster mother, but to the delight of the audience." On the other hand, ten-year-old Jean, settling into her new home in Windsor with other children of Ford Motor employees "quite enjoyed it when publicity brought us into the limelight." A young Canadian girl was so jealous of the attention given to a British evacuee living near her in Saskatoon that she locked herself in her bathroom for hours at a time to practice her British accent. Gradually, the interest faded and the guest children learned that "when the novelty wore off the true friends remained." The children, generally, seem to have enjoyed the publicity and many cut out their names and photographs from the newspapers to send home or to treasure themselves. For a few, however, the attention was disturbing, and childcare workers traced their adjustment difficulties to the early publicity. One boy was said to be restless and eager for attention for years after he arrived at the age of six because of "the publicity he received when he came to Canada," and more than one teenager was said to have been badly affected by the early attention.[20]

During the first weeks in their new homes it was often the minor differences that struck the children most vividly. They had to adopt new routines, cope with new foods and learn a new language. Meals were eaten at different times and under different names than at home: "lunch and supper rather than dinner and tea." The main meal was taken in the evening rather than the middle of the day. Don, for one, found that "the whole mode of life was different . . . the manner of dress, speech, food, eating methods."

The abundance offered in their new homes made a vivid impression on the children. For some, the quantities of food seemed excessive. Fifteen-year-old Peter thought "Canadians . . . very wasteful . . . whole uneaten breakfasts dumped into the garbage!" Dorothy reveled in what was offered: "We had more to eat such as milk and lovely tomatoes . . . sliced by the plateful. [Plus] lobsters, which were new to us." Some of the new foods did not appeal. One young boy refused to eat corn on the cob because it was "vulgar." Ten-year-old Dudley was taken aback by "strange new customs — sugar on tomatoes, marmalade on bacon, cheese on apple pie, peanut butter and mint jelly, corn on the cob, hot dogs, toasted marshmallows."

Just as the food was new, so was the language. One nine-year-old girl was "relieved to discover that Canadians spoke English. I hadn't been clear about this—but the vocabulary and accent did seem a bit odd at first." The younger children slipped into Canadian usage and adopted Canadian accents without too much thought. A six-year-old boy from the north of England could "at first . . . hardly be understood." By October 1941, he was "speaking very distinctly and possibly . . . his parent will find he has lost his brogue and they may have difficulty." By the time he was eight, in 1943, one boy's "big amusement [was] to make fun of the BBC announcers." Older children, in contrast, sometimes struggled to keep their accents out of a sense of loyalty to home. In one family, "the older girl tried to keep her English accent and the younger to lose it."

Perhaps the most complex question of language the guest children faced was what to call their foster parents. The question was a highly emotional one and most children went through a number of titles before settling on one they were comfortable with. Eight-year-old Jean was astonished to find herself among children who "called their father by his first name . . . they also said goddam and Jesus Christ!" Older children often called their foster parents Mr. and Mrs., and some never went beyond this formal usage. If they did, they were most likely to call their foster parents Aunt and Uncle. Nicknames were rarely used—although one teenaged boy called his foster parents "Auntie and the Boss" and some of the younger children used variations of baby talk such as "Nunkie." Children who were aged ten and older when they arrived in Canada were reluctant to take the emotional step of calling their foster parents Mum and Dad, and foster parents themselves may have been reluctant to encourage older children to do so. Among younger children, Mum and Dad were more commonly used, and at all ages a developing relationship was sometimes marked by a shift from Mr. and Mrs. or Uncle and Aunt to Dad and Mum.[21]

During the first weeks in their new homes, as they struggled with new manners and a new language, the children began to realize that they could be in Canada for a long time. George found it difficult "coming to terms with the fact that I was a long way from home and realizing it would be for a lot longer than I had been led to believe." Like most of the guest children, he suffered from bouts of homesickness especially at Christmastime. An eight-year-old girl was slower to realize what the future held. She found the first months in Canada fun because "I thought it was only going to be for a short time." Only after some time did she begin to miss the life she had known in England. No amount of warmth and affection in the foster homes could smother all uncertainty and homesickness. Even in the homes where the children settled quickly and established warm relations, the first weeks were marked by anxiety. One nine-year-old girl was so tension-ridden that she "vomited on the breakfast table every morning . . . too much for a nine-year-old girl to bear alone." Thirteen-year-old Phyllis was "very happy in the day but the nights were bad" and she cried herself to sleep for many weeks. "This distressed my foster mother who was kindness herself."

Children who were apparently free from homesickness and separation anxiety sometimes startled their foster parents with other signs of distress. Aggressive behavior was common. Jean, the eleven-year-old who had forced the authorities to find her a new home by refusing to leave her seat on the staircase, began a turbulent career with her new family when her foster mother stooped to kiss her goodnight for the first time. "No colonist is good enough to kiss me" she said, turning away her head. Boys could be particularly aggressive and demanding. An eleven-year-old boy in a nominated home was reported, in October 1940, to be "treating his foster mother as though she were expected to entertain and wait on him" and to have "ordered (her) to give him his English money to spend as he pleased and resented her refusal." Cheekiness, impudence, spitefulness, squabbling, quarreling and fighting were common among the guest children. Many new parents faced apparent coldness and real challenges from the guest children which they had not anticipated. The foster mother of one "saucy" thirteen-year-old girl wondered, as more than one parent did, "if she was too old to cope with [a] lively teenager." She stuck it out and made a home for the girl until she went back to Britain in 1944.[22]

It is easy to think of adjustment as a matter of the guest child learning to live with the foster family and to forget that the foster family also had to learn to live with the child. The sudden arrival of one or more children in a home affected the foster parents, the fosters brothers and sisters and, in some homes, the servants. One foster mother recalls that when her three guests arrived, "three of my four maids left immediately." She could find no one willing to replace the departed help and was suddenly called on to care for her home and the children with less help than she had been used to with a smaller family. While few foster families experienced that dramatic a change in their household arrangements, all had to make some adjustments. Some of the couples to whom children were nominated were in their seventies when the guests arrived in 1940. If they had no grown children living at home they often found it difficult to cope with a new generation of children and, in many cases, the children were later moved. There were exceptions. A girl who arrived in Canada at the age of eight spent the war happily with her grandparents once her grandfather recovered from the fact that she was "too talkative."

The guest children brought their own experience of family life into their new homes. It is clear, from the comments made at the time and from the reminiscences of the evacuees, that British children generally had fewer chores in their own homes than Canadian children. Farm children did more and heavier work than town children, but in either case, the guest children were soon given regular chores, which they sometimes resisted. Many foster parents were surprised to find that their foster children refused to take a paper route. In Canada, the paper route symbolized initiative and responsibility, qualities that made Prime Ministers. In England, delivering papers was seen by the children as a badge of poverty and a stigma to be avoided. There were often difficulties over daily routines. Some working-class children were used to being fed when they came home rather than coming home at a set time for meals. Childcare workers supported the foster parents when they insisted that children be on time for meals.

Guest children argued against rules setting aside time for homework and over the time when they had to be home. One Canadian recalls the discipline problems in her home when the guest child arrived. Her parents "found it difficult to have one set of rules for their own children and another for the British child" and insisted that all the children follow the same rules. "We don't do that in England" was a popular argument. A teenager refused to wear overshoes and a raincoat "saying he never did so in England." Young David "insisted that prayers could be said while lying in bed," and his foster father asked his father for "a ruling on this point" in a letter describing how the boy was settling in.[23]

The differences raised the question of discipline. Parents and childcare authorities agreed that children needed discipline but disagreed over what was acceptable and necessary. Older foster parents tended to keep a stricter discipline than did the younger ones. A nine-year-old girl, sent to live with an aunt and uncle whose children had grown, was "expected to be seen and not heard and I think my relatives found it difficult to have so young a child in the house again when their own were at university." Eight-year-old Yolande, the daughter of actors, lived with her retired aunt and found her "more English than the English! Regulated life, table manners, tea in the afternoon. She did not approve of what she called 'the free and easy modern ways'." Six-year-old Timothy was one of a group of Ford Motor employees' children who spent the war in the home of Ford Motor Company President W.R. Campbell in Windsor, Ontario. He recalls the strict Presbyterian atmosphere of the home and the emphasis on "Victorian attitudes to morals, money, manners, etc." The daughters of the family were in immediate charge of the children and maintained discipline with spankings and by washing out the children's mouths with soap when they lied. Timothy did not find the atmosphere oppressive and "loved every minute" of his time in the home. Some foster parents insisted on a strict discipline out of a sense of responsibility to the parents. Ten-year-old Jean and her brother "were very strictly brought up as Auntie said we must return to England as well-behaved as we arrived. Life was lived to a strict routine, more strict than home, but most of the time we were happy . . . we had home duties which were different than in England."

Most children, however, found life in Canada freer than in the homes they had left. While children were expected to do more about the house than in Britain, they were also treated more as equals than were children in Britain. Among younger Canadian parents of the 1930s there was a turning away from corporal punishment. A foster father wrote "our children have been reared *without ever* being touched in anger, there is small likelihood that a good boy like David will need any correctional measures of such an old fashioned type." Most guest children shared the experience of Patricia, who found that "everything was less formal and children were part of their parents' lives instead of being separate." Some guest children found it difficult to adjust to the new atmosphere of freedom. One eight-year-old girl, sent to live with a family with two girls a little older than herself, was "quite surprised at the lack of supervision over shopping for clothes by the two girls and their homework was never supervised." She felt "rather lost without some structured life at the age of eight but gradually got used to it."[24]

Canadian children were rarely consulted when their parents decided to take in a guest child. These strange children, speaking with odd accents, behaving in unusual ways and surrounded by publicity and public concern were suddenly dropped into the Canadian children's familiar world. They found themselves with new brothers and sisters who altered the family structure and could be competitors for their parents' affection. Some foster parents tried to reduce the potential for friction by choosing guests of different ages than their own children. One mother took in three children under ten, all much younger than her own children, "as I didn't think it was a wise thing to try to pair up with ours." The age spread did not always prevent friction. A ten-year-old girl, joining a family with a four-year-old boy, was "somewhat put about" by her new foster brother and resented not being the youngest in her family as she had been at home. She continued to "fight furiously" with her foster brother during the years she spent with the family and is now amazed at the tolerance they showed her, even taking her with them when they left Toronto to settle in a new town. There were bound to be clashes of personality between strong-willed guest children and their foster brothers and sisters. When eleven-year-old Jean, who found no colonist good enough to kiss, settled into her new home, her six-year-old foster sister found her "a nuisance" to be tolerated. The girls quarreled, and on one occasion the younger girl scratched Jean's face. Jean told her foster mother that the cat had made the scratch. Although never close as children, the two are now "like sisters."[25]

One source of friction in the early months was

money. CORB and the Canadian government had a long dispute over the money being paid by the children's parents in the summer of 1940. The Canadian government, like other Dominion governments, refused to accept money for the foster parents. Crerar was afraid that any suggestion of payment would affect the appeal for free homes. Unlike the other Dominions, however, the Canadian government did accept five shillings a week for each child for an emergency fund and a grant of £3 for each child to buy a winter outfit. While it took the money, the Canadian government insisted that no public announcement about the fund and the grant should be made, again from fear of the effect on the appeal for free care. Dr. Wallace went even further than that. In November 1940, he made an appeal on the radio for contributions to the National Advisory Committee but made no reference to the money being paid by CORB out of the weekly payments of the British parents. "While the children are with us they are Canadian children and Canadians have the responsibility for their care" Wallace intoned as he called for gifts from the generous-hearted people of Canada.

No issue caused more confusion and unhappiness in the first months of the evacuation than money. Some children arrived in Canada with the impression that their parents were paying for their keep and they took "for granted the many things which were given them merely as their just due." The children usually learned better as they settled in, but their parents and foster parents remained confused. If the money was not going to foster parents, what was it being used for? Were parents being asked to pay the transport costs of their children? The questions flew between parents, foster parents and officials as 1940 passed into 1941. An Ontario official reported in February 1941 that "questioning of what is being done with the money paid into the Evacuee Fund by British parents is still rife among our foster parents." They accepted the explanation that the money was going to defray the costs of CORB "and made no real complaints but . . . the parents in England do not know what is being done with the money. When told that not one cent of it comes to foster parents here, they ask why the payments have to be continued . . . a great deal of questioning passes between them and the parents in England."

CORB grew increasingly exasperated with the Canadian position which, as one official said, "appears to be misleading and to place the U.K. government in a false position." Maxse herself pointed out that there was increasing criticism in Britain of the failure to send money to foster parents. "The most urgent aspect is Canada. The Canadian Government has done less and obtained more than any other Dominion." The Federal government provided free transport in Canada and free education "but has not seen to the provision of clothes or even the school books and material for the education it offers. It has also been more exacting about standards of acceptance than the other Dominions." The protests from Britain eventually had an effect on the Canadian government. In March 1941, Crerar, on the urging of Blair, persuaded the Cabinet to join other Dominions and stop taking the five shillings a week. As the provinces and most of the foster parents had refused to draw on the fund for winter clothes, most of that money was returned to the United Kingdom. The weekly contributions were kept in Britain to meet the costs of CORB.[26]

Providing a home for a guest child was a financial strain for many families. The CWC estimated that it cost at least $250 a year to keep a child. The University of Toronto began by allowing $60 a month to each mother and child but soon raised the allowance to $85. In Montreal, the COS allowed a mother and child $15 a week. Finance Minister J.L. Ilsley agreed to amend the Income Tax Act in July 1940 to allow the foster parents of CORB children to qualify for income-tax relief. He thought this concession worth $50-$80 a child and it was the only concession he would make. Not even Prime Minister King could persuade Ilsley to grant similar relief to all Canadians giving a home to guest children. Only CORB children brought a tax benefit; private evacuees brought their foster parents no relief because the Minister feared that would "involve far reaching consequences in respect of dependents generally."[27]

The expenses feared most by foster parents were medical and dental bills. The evacuee children were generally very healthy, and life in Canada agreed with them. In the first year, many children grew at a pace that amazed observers. A.T. Proctor reported to Blair, as early as November 1940, that "the way these children have put on weight and grown since their arrival . . . is something which would astonish you. We have cases of children who have put on fifteen pounds . . . and grown four inches in height." The children grew more rapidly than average Canadian children and continued to make impressive gains during their stay. CORB found that the children sent to Canada grew more than those sent to the other Dominions. Serious illness was rare but many children did spend a short time in hospital, most commonly for tonsillectomy and adenoidectomy. Canadian doctors were quick to recommend the operation, and one study reported that a majority of all children in Toronto had their tonsils removed by the age of six. Maxse noted that "at one time it appeared as if no child would return with its tonsils." That was not quite the case, although on one day in November 1940, nine British children were in Toronto's Hospital for Sick Children for the operation. Nearly five percent of the CORB children in Ontario were operated on in their first year in Canada. While some British parents of private evacuees refused permission for the operation when it was recommended by a Canadian doctor, the childcare agencies generally agreed to it. The cost of hospital care for CORB children was met by the federal government, but foster parents had to pay the doctor or dentist. Medical and Dental Associations in 1940 encouraged their members to treat the children without charge, and most foster parents took the guest children to their family practitioners, many of whom did give the guests free treatment.[28]

The federal government did not assist private evacuees. Blair's comments about the alleged seven hundred stranded guests drew attention to the question in July 1940, and a number of organizations offered help. The CNCR, thwarted in its efforts to open the doors to European refugees, took responsibility for the foreign refugees who had managed to get into Canada and were now out of funds. Jewish philanthropic agencies helped Jewish mothers and children. The Federation of University Women aided graduate women and the Imperial Order of the Daughters of the Empire (IODE) volunteered to assist British mothers who were not covered by the other groups. The IODE made a levy on its members for the work and made payments to families referred to them by social agencies in the cities and provinces. At the peak of demand for help, late in 1941, the IODE gave money to fifty-six families in five provinces. Montreal was a special problem since, as the port of entry to Canada, some families were stranded there. The COS arranged help for forty families in 1940 from the different social agencies, and the Quebec government allowed the COS to spend public money on private evacuees. The number of women and children who needed help, however, was far below Blair's figure of seven hundred.[29]

When the government evacuation ended, Keith Jopson suggested that CORB should care for the private evacuees. He estimated that as many as half of the children might want to join the CORB scheme. Some members of the Executive of the National Advisory Committee were willing to take responsibility for all the children. They argued that even if they did so, the total number would still be less than the ten thousand first invited. Blair was appalled at the suggestion because it would "involve heavy expenditure by the Government" and it would also entitle the foster parents to claim an income-tax exemption at further cost to the government. Although his Minister, Crerar, was willing to approach the government, he was discouraged by Blair, who successfully resisted the suggestion of a general transfer of children to government responsibility. If the arrangements for a child broke down, he became a charge of the local CAS as a Canadian child would have in similar circumstances. The CAS would then approach the Immigration Branch to ask that the child be taken into government sponsorship. Blair rarely accepted the children because of the cost. He was particularly worried by the fact that government evacuees had a free passage home to Britain.

Blair always believed that "where the possibility of getting something from the Government is concerned, folks for the most part fall into one class, those with the outstretched hand." People had taken responsibility for the children and they should accept it. In practice, however, it was difficult to ignore the needs of children in trouble. Ontario took over supervision of 150 private evacuees in 1940 and maintained responsibility for about that number through the war. The federal government set up a fund to help children whose support had evaporated or whose foster families were suddenly faced with heavy medical bills. Childcare agencies investigated private evacuees at the request of their parents, although that sometimes brought a frosty response from foster parents who resented the intrusion into their private lives. The supervision of private evacuees in trouble was usually taken on by a provincial agency without transferring the child to the government scheme.[30]

The children arrived and settled into their new homes as the school year began in 1940. Dr. R.C. Wallace, as Chairman of the National Advisory

Committee, had no doubt that the guest children should go to public schools and that the Committee should not pay for children who had been sent to private schools. The public schools were willing to take in the children and school boards announced that the guest children would be treated as residents. With a pupil teacher ratio of 42:1, Toronto worried about the cost of opening classrooms and hiring extra teachers if thousands of children came into the city, but the Ontario government quickly offered to pay half the salaries if teachers had to be hired. The 439 guest children who entered Toronto schools that autumn, however, were absorbed at "practically no extra cost" and the guest children elsewhere put no measurable pressure on school systems. The *Globe and Mail* reported that the British children "as a general thing take higher standing than our children" because their training was "a little wider and perhaps a little more thorough than the training given here and . . . the British child has a somewhat broader knowledge." Back in England, *The Times* Educational Supplement was reassuring its anxious readers that in "intensiveness, interest and duration of schooling, facilities are in every way comparable to the best British standards."[31]

School offered one of the biggest contrasts with home for the guest children and, next to family and friends, was the greatest influence on their lives in Canada. The children left behind a highly selective educational system that offered the greatest opportunities to those with money. The fact that some guest children had left school even before 1940 points up the nature of the English system. In the last year before the war, only 14% of the children in state elementary schools went on to secondary school. In a typical year in the mid-1930s, only 10% of the youths beginning work were over sixteen years of age. Four children of every thousand in elementary schools reached university. The world of the British public school was almost inaccessible to working-class and lower-middle-class children. There had been plans to change the structure of British state education, to raise the school-leaving age and to build more schools, but they had been modified or set aside in the years of government restraint that preceded the depression of the 1930s. The great changes in British schools came only at the end of the war. The schools the guest children left behind were usually the old buildings of the nineteenth century, where large classes studied a traditionally academic curriculum emphasizing literature, mathematics, the classics, sciences and, to a lesser degree, modern languages. Discipline in the schools was firm, relations between staff and pupils distant and formal, and single-sex schools the norm. Many of the children were nervous about entering school in Canada. For a year before leaving home, the war had interrupted their education and some had attended overcrowded schools with disrupted schedules, staff shortages and a shortened school day.

In Canada, the 1920s and 1930s had seen growing attendance at high schools and a decline in the selectivity of the system. By the 1920s, a majority of English-Canadian teenagers were in high school. There was considerable interest in curriculum reform, and most provinces offered a core of subjects and a range of electives. In a number of provinces, the different types of high school were merged into composite secondary schools, where students from a wide variety of social backgrounds mixed. There was much talk of the social goals of the high school and changes were being made to emphasize child-centered education. The emphasis on examinations and selectivity began to decline as recommendations replaced examinations. It was a sharp contrast with Britain.[32]

The sharpest contrast of all, however, was between the urban British school and the rural Canadian. The guest children who lived on farms found themselves back in the days of the one-room schoolhouse. They had to learn to ride to school and put their horse in the barn in the summer or ride in the cutter with their foster brothers and sisters in the winter. The schools they attended were often one room heated by a wood-burning stove. Students were grouped together — perhaps Grades 7–11 in one group or "anywhere from 1-8 grades in a class." Eight-year-old Peter went from the London suburbs to a farm in British Columbia eight miles away from his school, where eight grades occupied two rooms. It was "a vast change" but one he accepted easily. A guest child found it "*very* odd to have everyone in one room. The students in Grade 9 looked like grown men and women to me." Many children shared that first reaction at seeing such old people in their classroom, but the guest children adapted easily to these small rural schools and were usually promoted to grades beyond their age.

Most guest children did not ride to a one-room schoolhouse, but biked or walked to the local school in a Canadian town. Crowds of curious children greeted the British boys and girls on their first morning in the schoolyard. The papers had been full of stories about the children all summer and the Canadian children were eager to hear the curious accents and find out how the guest children liked Canada. The guests experienced a fresh burst of attention. Peter was a curiosity because of his accent and his "strange British clothes" but the interest soon faded. It helped to have a friend to introduce you to the ways of the schoolyard, just as it helped in the neighborhood. Nine-year-old Jean, entering a school in Moose Jaw, was put in charge of a classmate who remains her friend to this day. Gladys was taken to North Toronto Collegiate by a girl from the house next door who "treated me like a sister" and helped her through an experience she had approached with anxiety. A nine-year-old girl who had been through a number of personal crises and "at this stage of a disturbed childhood [would] probably have had difficulty socializing anywhere" was helped in making a difficult adjustment by a neighborhood child who had been asked to take care of her "and [who] never deserted me" even when some of the other children "shunned" her. George found that he was quickly accepted by his classmates because his foster brother was very popular at school. A sixteen-year-old, returning to school after being at work for a couple of years in England, was struck by the relations between the boys at his school. He found the older boys brotherly toward the younger ones — "a marked contrast to my experiences in England."

The children quickly settled into the life of the school. One of the first things they wanted was to dress like their classmates. Adam and Duncan came home from their first day at a rural Manitoba school and demanded "long pants. I thought the gray flannel shorts looked so nice but one day at school was enough to convince Duncan that they were too 'different.' So to town we went and black denim covered the sturdy Scottish knees." Not all the guest children succumbed to Canadian fashion. In Victoria, a group of English schoolgirls wore their English uniforms until they grew too small. The demands for acceptable clothes were, perhaps, intensified by the fact that Canadian schools were coeducational. Tina thought it was "great that there were both *boys* and girls in class" and Margot was "dazzled by the idea of boys in class." Some of the girls were less comfortable with this social atmosphere; one found the "pupils rather precocious. The girls were *very* self regarding, make-up, hair, boy friends, possessions" and a thirteen-year-old felt uncomfortable with the "emphasis on lipstick and going steady at a very early age." Yolande noticed the emphasis on clothes and looking good: "I was amazed that the classes were mixed. The girls seemed very 'grown up' and self confident and were very concerned about clothes—I was used to school uniforms." Twelve-year-old Elspeth's "first valentine came from a Canadian boy." The boys, to judge from their recollections, were less struck by the presence of girls in the classroom.

Both boys and girls were astonished by the age range of the children in their classes. Urban schools did not combine a number of grades in one class, as did rural schools, but they did hold back children who failed a grade. Age difference also affected many of the guest children because of the custom of accelerating academically talented children through the school. Guest children, especially those who had been attending grammar schools, tended to do well on tests and to be advanced a grade or two after being tested in Canada. This was not a universal practice. George was "slightly put out at being put in Grade 8 and being made to take the High School entrance exam" even though he had passed the grammar school entrance before leaving Britain. Ten-year-old Mike, at school in Sherbrooke, was kept with his age group despite his requests to go up. As he found the work in Canada two years behind what he had done in England, he coasted along at the top of his class. George and Mike may have been more fortunate than they realized. The guest children who were advanced were sometimes unhappy. They found that they had to adjust to being in a strange country and a difficult social situation. An eleven-year-old boy was the youngest child in his Grade 8 class, "which made it a bit tough on top of being new to the country." It was a common experience for guest children in 1940 to be younger by a couple of years than their classmates. Children in elementary schools, however, were less likely to be pushed ahead. Over the years, the younger guest children generally advanced with their Canadian contemporaries and were less likely to feel like oddities.

Teachers were very interested in the guest children in their first days at school and sometimes singled them out for special attention. Children were often called on whenever the teacher felt that a comparison with Britain was useful for the class. Nine-year-old Joyce so impressed her teacher with her reading skills that she was taken from room to room to read to the other teachers. Some teachers were especially solicitous of the guest children because of the disruptions they had suffered or because they thought of them as symbols of the Old Country. Special attention of any kind, however, tended to make the child's adjustment to school more difficult. Don found that his first teacher "was too deferential at first but I think she soon realized it was creating problems with our peers and school-mates."

Corporal punishment was common in Canadian schools for lateness and other misdemeanors, and one guest recalls that "I had my share," but Canadian classrooms were not as regimented as those in Britain. The guest children enjoyed the very different relationship between teachers and students. Canadian teachers were more approachable and more helpful than the ones they had left. "In England I spoke when I was spoken to, in Canada students spoke when they felt like it." Many guest children were amazed and pleased to find that Canadian teachers seemed willing to spend time helping the children with any special problems. Adam is sure that he would not have received the same level of education in Scotland "where teachers did not have the same time to devote to each pupil" as in his rural school. Even in the large city schools, Canadian teachers were ready to take an interest in their students. Tony and his twin brother were "treated as something really special" by their teachers, who later phoned to welcome them when they returned to Winnipeg shortly after the war.

In a few of the larger towns — Montreal, Vancouver, Windsor — guest children were present in large enough numbers to form groups. In Montreal, the Penguin Club was organized to arrange summer holidays and put on an annual play by the children. In Windsor, the children of Ford Motor Company employees were a visible presence in the schools. For the most part, however, the guests blended into the life of the school, where the pressure to join the group in dress, speech and manners speeded their Canadianization. The guest children often felt most Canadian at school ceremonies, such as the citizenship or patriotic exercises required by most provinces during the war. School organizations and school friends were the focus of their social life outside the home and church. Jean recalls that "when we joined the Canadian Junior Red Cross at school, I figured I must be a Canadian because I was invited to join same as everyone else."[33]

Not all British children were in public schools. Hundreds began the school year in their own British school transferred to Canada or as students in a Canadian private school. The largest group to come to Canada with their school were the 160 children and staff of St. Hilda's, from Whitby in Yorkshire. The school was run by an Anglican order, the Sisters of the Holy Paraclete, and the party arrived in Montreal in the summer of 1940. They spent the late summer weeks at Ontario Ladies College in Whitby, Ontario, while their sponsors desperately scrambled to find accommodation and funds for the school. The Anglican community in Ontario rallied to the school following an appeal by Archbishop Owen of Toronto and Dr. Cosgrave, the head of Trinity College. Mrs. Watson Evans offered her country house, which stood in ninety acres of grounds at Erindale, near Toronto. Trinity College offered to advance operating funds, and by the opening of the school year, the house at Erindale had been equipped to take seventy of the girls. The furniture and household equipment was lent to St. Hilda's by people in the community. As the house was too small to take all the girls, the sisters arranged for twenty to go to Alma College in St. Thomas, eighteen to Bishop Strachan in Toronto and the balance returned to Ontario Ladies College. The staff at St. Hilda's made arrangements to bring the girls back together in 1941 by placing the youngest girls in a second country house with the older girls taking courses in Toronto while keeping the middle school at Erindale. By then, some of the girls were quite happily settled in their Canadian schools and chose not to return to St. Hilda's.

Without a group of sponsors, a British school in Canada could run into serious difficulties. Lady Eden brought her school of about twenty children to Canada in 1940 and led them to Vernon, British Columbia. There they spent six months at St. Michael's school before Lady Eden decided that the school facilities did not meet her needs and moved the group to Breakeyville, Quebec. The Breakey family allowed Lady Eden the use of Chaudière House. Some of the older girls left to attend school in Montreal and the rest of the children lived a hand-to-mouth existence with no money from Britain before 1942. By 1943, Lady Eden had had enough and decided that it was impossible to keep the school going. She declared it closed in the summer of 1943, and the children made their way back to Britain via Lisbon.

Most children who came to Canada with their schools entered into the life of the Canadian residential school that sponsored them. This, after all, was the justification for the work of the National Committee of Education and the reason for Major Ney's enthusiasm. The British children sometimes formed a separate group within the Canadian school. When the girls from St. Hilda's went to Alma College, they lived for a year in St. Hilda's House until Principal P.S. Dobson decided to incorporate the girls "into the general life of the school." He assured the parents that the girls' religious life would continue to be guided by the sisters of St. Hilda's. At Branksome Hall, a group of girls from Sherborne School in Dorset kept a degree of separateness under the charge of Miss Diana Reader Harris. A group of fifty girls from Roedean spent the war years with two of their teachers at Edgehill School in Windsor, Nova Scotia. Smaller groups of children attended private schools scattered across Canada.

The host schools made special financial arrangements for the British children to keep costs close to what the parents paid in Britain. Ashbury College, in Ottawa, offered a special rate of $500 to the parents of British boys for most of the war. The schools, however, faced the problem that no money could be sent out of Britain. Concessionary fees had to be paid by local supporters of the schools or alumni until the blocked funds were freed from Britain. Support for the Roedean girls was so great at Edgehill that a surplus of $5,000 became available when funds were released by the British after the war. It was used for a scholarship to commemorate the connection.

The arrival of a group of British children in a school often had a stimulating effect on the Canadian children. The principal of Edgehill noted that "some of the visitors were outstanding students and all had reached a good standard for their ages. The Canadians did not want to be beaten and never worked harder in their lives." At Branksome Hall, Miss Reader Harris noted a similar effect and took the opportunity to praise the Canadian girls: "An influx of energetic English girls has meant that some of the prizes for work and games have passed to the English girls. The ready generosity of those who but for this influx would have gained the prizes has been very marked."

As boarding-school pupils, these guest children had already undergone a separation from their parents that eased the move to Canada. At their Canadian schools, they were generally accepted easily, although they might be teased as one girl was "until I grew several inches and adopted a Canadian accent." A number of them recall that they were easily accepted because they all shared the experience of being away from home: "Our mutual circumstances were more alike than if I had gone to public school" as one points out. The teachers were usually sympathetic and some were British themselves, which the children found comforting. Some of the residential schools in Ontario still emphasized a British link. At Branksome Hall, the girls wore kilts and were organized into Clans, not Houses. Each term opened with a Clan games which broke the ice and allowed the Sherborne girls to feel they belonged. At Branksome Hall, too, the staff encouraged the girls to remember "their English traditions" while entering into the life of the Canadian school. Miss Harris reported that the girls "are able to be loyal and enthusiastic members of two schools at once."[34]

As the guest children began the new school year, uninterrupted by air raids and broken school days, the first phase of the evacuation was ending. The reception centers were closed and the staffs discharged when it was clear that thousands of children would not arrive in 1940. The seven thousand guest children in Canada would be joined by a few hundred private evacuees in 1941, but there would be no further mass evacuation. Most children were settled in the home in which they would live until it was time to return. No one knew when that would be and the parents, the foster parents and the children all gradually came to realize that the evacuation was not a short-term escape from the immediate danger of blitz and invasion. In the phrase of the time, most of the children were in Canada "for the duration."

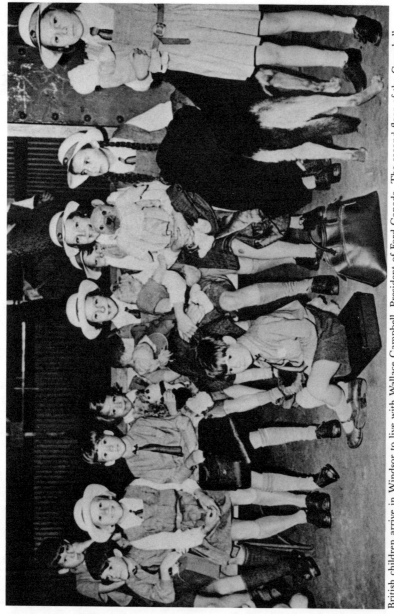

British children arrive in Windsor to live with Wallace Campbell, President of Ford Canada. The second floor of the Campbell home was converted into a dormitory for the children. 1940. (Windsor Star Library)

British children waiting to be transported to foster homes across Canada. 1940. (Toronto Telegram Collection, York University Archives)

Parents waiting in line at the Passport Office in London to arrange travel documentation for their children. 1940. (Toronto Telegram Collection, York University Archives)

Children of English Electric Company officials arrive in Canada to be guests of the company's Canadian representatives. 1940. (Toronto Telegram Collection, York University Archives)

British children eating breakfast in Montreal. Some of the children were placed with families in the city while the others journeyed to Toronto, Winnipeg, and Vancouver. 1940. (Toronto Telegram Collection, York University Archives)

Children return to Britain after their ship was torpedoed while crossing the North Atlantic Ocean on its way to Canada. None of the children was injured. 1940. (Toronto Telegram Collection, York University Archives)

British children from Scotland and England arrive at Union Station in Toronto. 1940. (Toronto Telegram Collection, York University Archives)

British school girls at Union Station in Toronto. 1940. (Toronto Telegram Collection, York University Archives)

Sir Winston S. Churchill. (National Archives of Canada)

William Lyon MacKenzie King. (National Archives of Canada)

Hon. Thomas Alexander Crerar. (National Archives of Canada)

Frederick Charles Blair. (National Archives of Canada)

Fred J. Ney. (National Archives of Canada)

Charlotte Whitton. (National Archives of Canada)

Carine Wilson. (National Archives of Canada)

Sir Geoffrey H. Shakespeare. (National Portrait Gallery. London, England)

CHAPTER VI

❖

BRAVE YOUNG STRANGERS

❖

JOHN HUTTON: Age 7
CORB Evacuee

John settled easily into his second family. He made a special friend of his young foster sister, an open and trusting four-year-old. She was always able to cheer him up when he felt low during the years in Agincourt. He copied Doris and began to call his foster mother Mummy. Mrs. Pellett had "suggested Auntie but that just didn't suit him." By early June, John decided that Mummy was a little babyish and he began to call Mrs. Pellett Mother. He kept his two fathers separate in his own mind by calling his father "my Daddy" and his foster father "our Daddy." He soon grew to like his foster brother, and his foster mother wrote that "they have a grand time together and he seems to be living a normal child's life by having a sister to tease and a brother to scrap with. I must say though that the scraps are few and far between and of very little importance." John also wrote to his father along similar lines: "Doris is a fairly good girl."

School was still in when John moved to Agincourt and he soon joined in the classes and activities — playing in the Rhythm Band at parents' night and joining a growing circle of friends who would stick with him all the time he was in Canada. He ate "three hearty meals a day," which his mother took to be a sign of health. The local doctor, however, thought him nervous and high-strung and felt that eating was one sign of his nervousness. By January, John's father commented that he "looks a beefy lad" in the Christmas photos, and in later years his foster mother worried about his weight.

There was an underlying tension to those first weeks of adjustment. It showed clearly early in June when John's father was one of the parents chosen to send a message by radio to their children overseas. Mrs. Pellett described the broadcast. "Well, we all certainly had a great thrill last evening when he heard you broadcasting direct from England. It came over the shortwave. I did not have a shortwave set so a very kind lady in the village brought her set right over to our place so that John could hear you without going into a strange home to do so. We got it fairly clearly but there is to be a re-broadcast over the Canadian Broadcasting System on Sunday June 8th and we are looking forward very much to hearing that. John was a brave little boy when he heard you. When the announcer gave your name out, my, it was wonderful to see the beautiful expression and lovely smile break out on John's face. When you had finished speaking he quite filled up with tears but he would not let himself cry. It was all I could do to keep from crying myself." John wrote "I heard you on the shortwave radio and I am going to hear you again. I have a book that tells how far the nearest star is away from us. I am going to ask you some questions and see if you know. The answers will be on a little piece of paper."

When school began again, John ran into some trouble. He was inattentive in class. In November, John had to write home sending his report card with the note that "the d in conduct means too much talking." His foster mother had talked to the teacher, who explained that John's behavior was generally good but that "in the middle of the lesson he would suddenly think of something and start right away to tell his neighbor about it. She has kept him in at recess many times but still he doesn't pay attention to her and keeps talking." Mrs. Pellett put it down to the fact that "he has had a great many changes in the past eighteen months" and only needed some security and guidance to "straighten him out and eventually we will." His foster mother also felt that part of his trouble at school came from the fact that his teacher was newly qualified and "I doubt if she knows much about child psychology and John is one who needs understanding."

John kept getting into trouble with his teacher and was kept in after school most days. Though they tried not to talk about the war in front of him, his foster parents could tell that he was worried about his father. When news came that Mr. Hutton would probably have to leave Colchester, John blurted out "I wish he didn't have to leave. I'm afraid." He was soon in more trouble at school for daydreaming and inattentiveness, and it was clear to his foster mother that he constantly worried about the war. News from home about the war and about his father being told to prepare for call up made him physically ill, and in March 1942, his foster parents took him into the Sick Children's Hospital for a physical examination and a consultation at the Neurological Clinic. All the doctors could do was confirm Mrs. Pellett's own diagnosis that John "was worrying about the war and there is little we can do about it." Every time a letter came from home John was quick to check that it still came from Colchester.

Mr. Hutton's work was defined as war work and the possibility that he would be called up receded in 1942. John's health improved and he grew so content that his foster mother wished "he would be a little more mischievous" and not quite such an obedient child "for he does not seem to have a scrap of mischief in him." School grew a little easier, and church groups, Cubs and playing with his large circle of friends kept John busy and apparently happy. A family friend serving with the RAF in Canada dropped in on the Pelletts, and he wrote to Colchester to say John "looks fine and boy oh boy what an accent." Soon after, however, John fell ill again when Mr. Pellett had to leave his job and look for another. It was a time of anxiety for the family, and there was the possibility that they might have to leave Agincourt. John developed a fever and stomach troubles that put him in bed on more than one occasion. Mr. Pellett found a new job, Mr. Hutton wrote to say that he had bought a house in Colchester "because I wanted a place for you to come back to after the war" and John recovered.

John still kept his feelings closely guarded, as his foster mother noticed when Mr. Hutton made a second broadcast from London early in 1943. "Last Thursday we heard over the radio — shortwave — your voice and are looking forward to hearing you again on our own radio. It was very clear. Really, one would think you were sitting in the same room. We didn't miss a word. John said it sounded just like you. He was sure thrilled, but he keeps his feelings to himself. Bobby and Doris appear to be more excited but I doubt it. John said afterwards, 'My, I felt funny in my stomach.' He did not feel blue this time though; not as he felt when you spoke before." John wrote "Today I heard you over the radio. You said you would like to hear the Grand Howl. If you come to Canada you could come to Cubs and stay and watch the Grand Howl and the games. Today I was walking on some snow and fell in. The water only went up to my socks. There is no news today. Today is Doris's birthday. I got a wolf's head cut out. My six is making the head. I know the reef knot, sheet bend, clove hitch and bowline. Doris is sick today. We had a bad snow storm. Daddy had to stay in the city. I forgot to tell you I went to the rink on Saturday. They put on music. I can skate pretty well."

The broadcasts and the steady stream of letters from his father kept him aware of home, and even as he grew to be a part of the gang in Agincourt, John never lost the sense that he was English and "that when the war was over I would be returning to England." As he grew older and more secure in his Canadian home, the illnesses disappeared and he settled into his schoolwork. His grades improved and he was passed into Grade 6 "without having to take his final exams.

Only the very best pupils get out of writing their finals" his foster mother proudly wrote. In what was to be his last summer in Canada, he was happy to work in the garden, which he had never done before, and to earn money to go to camp with Bobbie. There he learned to swim "about 12 yds., swim on my back for 47 seconds and do the duck dive. I feel fine, do you?"

Just as he seemed to gain some contentment, however, a new worry broke in. The summer of 1944 brought good news from Europe as the Allies pushed their campaign against the Germans. Victory was talked of everywhere, and with victory came thoughts of home. John's mood changed. "For the most part he is in very good spirits. Of late he seems to me to have been a little moody or quieter perhaps. I may be wrong but I feel it is the prospect of going back to England. With the war going the way it is, we feel it won't be so very long now and while he is most anxious to return to England and you I think he is rather loathe to leave Canada and his associations here. He says practically nothing about it but the situation is bound to be just about equally as difficult for him as when he left England. I feel better knowing that he has a father with the understanding you possess to return to. But oh, it is going to be difficult to let him go, and Bobbie and Doris are going to lose a brother who is very dear to them."

John did not go home before the new school year began, and that meant passing another milestone, which Mrs. Pellett reported. "We got John a new suit a week ago and I do not know what you are going to think or feel for we had to get him long pants. He looks very nice in them but so grown up. It gave me a queer feeling when he dressed and I couldn't help wondering how you will feel when you see him coming home in long trousers. He is sure going to be nice looking for he has such a lovely complexion and such lovely blue eyes. Bobbie and Doris are growing up fast too. Bob is quite tall but thin whilst Doris is like a young colt; she seems nothing but two legs.

"I thought I might tell you of the evening John first tried on his new suit. You should have been there. He got me into his room and shut the door so no one else would intrude and got me to watch him sit down and get up half a dozen times to see if he did it right. It was killing but I dare[d] not laugh. The first time he sat down he very daintily took hold of the side seam of the trousers with thumb and forefinger and carefully lifted them in the same manner as a lady in olden days might lift her skirt. He practiced for a while until I assured him he looked natural. But I could not help feeling that you should have been there. He is very self-conscious and needs the assurance that everything is just right for him. But everything seems to go wrong. At school yesterday he wore them for the first time."

The school year was marked by rumors of going home, but despite the false starts John stayed much calmer than he had been in his early days in Agincourt. In May 1945, Mrs. Pellett wrote: "I have some very good news for you and that is by the time you receive this letter John may well be on his way to England. I believe he is to be one of the first to go and it will likely be very very soon. Some who are trying their entrance examinations at school are not able to go until that is over but I talked with John's teacher and she said he will get his year's work even if he does not stay for his final exams. John is very happy over the thought of returning. I am very glad that he feels that way and I do [hope] that England will not be too strange to him after his long stay in Canada, and that he will feel quite happy and satisfied there. They tell me that so many of the older children are rebellious about returning home and I feel that is too bad, especially for their parents.

"Prepare yourself for meeting a very very big boy, Fred. There is no stopping his growing and he is quite stout. I am hoping he will lose some of that as he grows into his teens though. He is 5 feet 2 inches and weighs 130 lbs. His face has not changed much though so I am sure you will know him.

"It is ten o'clock and the boys are still talking in their room. John learned today that he is really going home tomorrow. They are quite excited. Bobby is torn between two emotions; one that he will miss John greatly and the other that he will have a bedroom of his own at last. I'm sure I do not know what he will do in that bedroom all alone for at bedtime they are at their chummiest. For over a year now they have not been nearly so close as chums. John has got over the playing stage and does not do so much of it. But Bobby still tears around and is not satisfied unless he is out of doors and playing somewhere."

Months would pass, however, before John finally left for home at the end of July 1945. He left behind many friends he remains in touch with and an understanding foster family who cared for him with such success that, looking back, he forgets the anxieties and the bouts of illness brought on by tension and recalls the years in Agincourt as "a happy interlude in my life."

NINA LAVILLE: Age 11
CORB Evacuee

The community of Steeldale had known hard times. It was homestead country, and many of the families were first-generation settlers, mostly Finns, who had struggled to make a living during the 1930s' drought. While Nina lived on her uncle's farm "we had several years with crop failures. Money was never very plentiful but I never went without anything that was important." It was a mixed farm with grain, livestock and chickens, and a big garden beside the house. One of the first things that struck Nina was "how *very* well my Uncle and Aunt ate. Not that we didn't have enough to eat in England — but being on a farm we had home-grown vegetables, butter, cream. Collecting the eggs was my job. Having chicken almost *weekly* — we only had it at Christmas in England. Being on a farm we were pretty well self-sufficient."

Nina's cousin was three years old and newly adopted by her parents. "I treated her like a doll, she liked me well enough although a little jealous always but that was natural. My Uncle Mark was delighted to have me — I think Aunty Betty was a bit apprehensive initially but when she saw how adaptable I was we got on famously. Everyone without exception was *so* kind, particularly my Aunt and Uncle. It must have been traumatic for them suddenly to have an eleven-year-old child dumped on them — what if I had been homesick or even a juvenile delinquent?" In either case, the Evacuee Bureau in Regina could have offered little help. A year went by between Miss Phin's visits to the farm.

In the midst of the small community, Nina felt herself "the darling of everybody. I was thoroughly spoiled by everyone — School, Church, Ladies Aid, the community in general. I loved them and they loved me." Even in her first days on the farm, she felt as if she had arrived where she belonged. Life revolved around work on the farm and play with the neighbor children who were intrigued by their visitor: "I was a novelty, the little English girl. I was unique. I learned to ski the first winter and also to ice skate on the neighbor's dam. I did rather disgrace myself the first time by trying to put my skates on *over* my shoes. Snowshoes were too clever for me. The snow and ice were novelties to be enjoyed without reservation and being 'snowed in' was just another delight to be experienced."

School was a four-mile walk away "or if the horses were not being used on the farm we rode. Wintertime we used a cutter." Gopher Hill School was "unbelievable — this funny little wooden shack with the little school house attached and the big barn out the back for the horses. Everyone in the same room with the big wood-burning stove. Only one teacher at first — Jean McDonald and then Ellen Tapanila. . . . school on the prairie [seemed] just one big happy family." The children made friends with her at once and called her Nina or "little Pierre" because of her French name.

High school was not as enjoyable. Because there was no high school in Steeldale, when it was time to go into Grade 9 Nina left the farm and moved into the nearby town of Dinsmore, where she stayed with friends of her foster parents during the school year. "I'm afraid I wasn't very academic—I'd rather do dramatics or debating. Maths, Physics, Chemistry were a complete mystery to me but History, Languages, English I adored." Life in Canada was absorbing and Nina felt thoroughly at home in the west. She wrote every week to her parents in Middlesborough, and they "sent a cablegram once a month. They all spoke on the wireless to me once." As she grew older, Nina's memory of her parents grew fainter. She began to feel that they were remote: "Just people I wrote to."

DAVID BROWN: Age 8
Rotary Evacuee

David returned from his vacation in 1940 to rejoin the Lukes. He now had a chance to notice "the differences in style between my own family and my host family." The Lukes were more easygoing than his sister's host family, and weekly Sunday School at the nearby Anglican church replaced the daily prayers and bible readings. The Lukes enjoyed an occasional drink; the Browns were teetotalers. "The family dynamics were different—generally there was more antagonism. . . . My own family worked by consensus." Nonetheless, David slipped easily into the routine of his new family and many of the differences between Browns and Lukes only became clear to him when he went home to Britain.

Morley had returned from camp by the time David came home from the Gaspé. The two boys shared a room and hit it off well. David sent a map of the room to his mother, showing himself in bed under a picture of Mrs. Brown while Morley snored away on the other side of the room. "Do you still sleep in the shelter or where do you sleep? We can sleep peacefully without mmmmmm and boom." David made friends quickly once school started, and enjoyed his Cub pack's weekly meetings. In his first winter, he learned to skate, and he and Morley built an igloo in the front yard. In January 1942, he told his mother "Today I would have played Cub hockey with some Cubs who live in Montreal West if I could only skate well enough and knew how to play." By 1943, such games were familiar stuff.

The Lukes wrote that "the Public School system of Britain is not in vogue here, but the West End schools [which] David and Janette will attend this fall are filled with the children of the people who live in these portions of the city—the residential English-speaking suburbs." David, like the Lukes's own children, attended a local school where "some of the women teachers seemed to have a soft spot for the English child." Early in 1941, he wrote to his mother: "A few days ago I was playing with a boy from Grade 4 and he said that I could read better than some pupils in his grade." In a spelling test "I got 100. It was simple."

The Lukes and Jan's foster parents were acquaintances but did not move in the same circles. As a result, David and his sister saw less of each other as time passed. In their first year in Canada, there were special efforts to bring them together for parties and celebrations, but it took a lot of arranging. "She lived in Westmount and we were supposed to see each other once a month. In practice I made about four visits a year to Westmount. She rarely visited me because it was not felt appropriate for her to travel alone." Increasingly, David and Jan moved inside the social boundaries of their respective foster families, and in the second summer in Canada, Jan returned to Metis Beach without David. He went instead to camp, and wrote to tell his mother that "I am all excited about it. Morley went two years ago and so he told me what you do." That summer, David learned to swim.

David felt a part of the Luke family and called his foster parents Mom and Dad. He was never made to feel that he was a burden to them, even when money grew tighter. As Mr. Luke's business declined and taxes rose, David "was aware that my host family were feeling the pinch and I later learned that my parents had only been able to send nominal support." Secure with the Lukes, he "always felt at home in Canada (that is, I never felt like a foreigner but equally always was aware that I was English.)" The Lukes tried to keep David in touch with his parents by insisting that he write home regularly. "Weekly letters home were enforced by my foster parents with a tenacity that I can only admire as a parent myself." His foster parents also took great pains to ensure that David "was always aware of my family and home in England."

In his early years in Montreal, homesickness surfaced from time to time. In one letter, David wrote, "I am having lots of fun over here but I would rather be back in England. I sometimes listen to the news from England." Later, he wrote, "I wish you and all my relations were here, as we have lots of fun, only you get homesick. We had that word in spelling and a boy wrote a sentence 'When I am at school I get homesick'! But the only thing that makes me homesick is music." His mother wrote regularly and sent him useful gifts as her way of contributing to his keep. Once, David flatly wrote to her "I do not want you to send me any more sweaters, socks and mitts."

In December 1944, Mr. Brown received an airmail letter from Montreal. Ted Davis, Chairman of the Guests of Canada Committee of the Rotary Club of Montreal, wrote that "in view of the great change in conditions which has taken place in the Old Country since the black days of 1940, we have been wondering whether the time has not now come when we should be considering their return." Davis asked Mr. Brown to request that David and Janette return to Britain, which was the first step to securing an exit permit for them. Mr. Brown immediately cabled the foster parents asking them to send the children home "as soon as convenient."

MARY ANN WAGHORN: Age 7
CORB Evacuee

"Dear Mummie I hope you are well. I am having a nice holiday. I have a big brother Teddy. He has a dog named Sport. I am very happy. I was on a big boat on the sea. I got three new frocks. Uncle Roly brought me a new book to look at. Uncle Roly is nice. I am at Canada. I have a big bed to sleep in. I like it in Canada. I will go to school soon." Mary Ann sat down to write home just as she had said she would. She wrote much the same letter to her father, concluding "this is the end of my nice and happy letter."

Aunt Coral, as she called Mrs. Mann, sensed that Mary Ann "is a child that needs to be loved," and the

Manns quickly surrounded her with affection. Teddy, her foster brother, "took me under his wing and only now, on reflection, can I appreciate his tolerance. If there was any degree of resentment or jealousy on the part of my brother I was never aware of it. A twelve-year-old boy might well have felt a bit put upon, even embarrassed before his friends, suddenly to have a degree of responsibility for a mere seven-year-old and a girl at that. He carted me off skating, taught me to fish, row a boat and it was only to please Ted that I forced myself to bait my own hooks with worms for fishing!" Mrs. Mann wrote: "She told us the other day that she is coming back to Canada when she is twenty and will marry him." Mary Ann quickly made friends in the neighborhood. "Almost without exception I was quickly befriended by classmates and neighboring children. Doubtless this was initially because I was something of an oddity or their parents had said that they should be kind to me. . . . This friendliness continued throughout the five years so must have been sincere. I have no recollection of being teased or made to feel an outsider."

"She told us about her people from time to time but right from the start she seemed to settle down as one of us" her foster father recalls. Mary Ann's Aunt Cis called often to take her out for the day, and while Mary Ann was glad to see her, she felt closer to Mrs. Mann and her Canadian family. "Although there must have been changes I don't recall noting any differences at the time. I feel I must have been encouraged to take my time and not rushed into situations which may have been new and strange." In her first weeks at Leaside, she began to put on weight and to lose the gaunt look she had after the long trip.

But the separation from home and the long weeks in Hart House did leave a mark. A month after Mary Ann arrived in Toronto, Mrs. Mann wrote: "One of us said 'what will we do this afternoon?' Mary said 'Let's take a big boat and go home to England.' . . . She speaks of you so much—but little brick that she is has never shown us that she is lonely." Mary Ann decorated an early letter home with a picture of a girl skipping and saying 'I want Mum' to another child who is laughing at her. In a later letter, she drew a similar picture with a baby in a pram saying 'I want Mummy' while a bigger child says 'Silly baby.' These feelings troubled her through Christmas 1940, and she welcomed her familiar toys from home. "I was glad to see my dolls from home. Mary's eyes fell out but Uncle Roly and Uncle Curry fixed them" she told her parents in a thank-you letter.

Gradually the round of activities and growing group of friends "Canadianised" Mary Ann. "I never felt that I *must* conform—one couldn't help it happening. I believe I probably became as Canadian outwardly as any of my friends, but was not allowed to forget that I was English, which I can now see was very sound. I don't mean, of course, that this was thrust at me constantly but they were so good not to let me lose sight of the fact that I would be going home one day."

The Manns wanted to inform Mary Ann about what was happening in Britain without frightening her. When she was first with them, they never listened to war news on the radio in case Maidstone was mentioned. But as she grew older, they encouraged her to take an interest in what was happening at home, and one summer she ran a bazaar with some friends and raised $10.56 for the *Evening Telegram*'s British War Victims Fund. The Manns ensured that she maintained her links with her own family: "Frequent letters, cables, postcards, photos, once a homemade record which a friend's father produced for me to send home" all helped her to feel in touch with home.

THE CURTIS FAMILY
CORB Evacuees

The three homes in which the Curtis children lived were very different. Hazel's foster father was a factory supervisor and they lived modestly without a car in one of Winnipeg's suburbs. They had volunteered to take a guest child "partly as war effort, partly [as] company for their daughter." Hazel "found it difficult to settle with one other girl after our large family at home, but soon got on very well with her. The only drawback was she was naturally brilliant at school and I found it hard to study enough to keep up with her." Her new home "was very warm with central heating" and Hazel noticed many other small differences — meal times for example — as she settled in. "It took the whole first year to realize the many differences."

Fred and Muriel's family were older than Hazel's, and their foster father was retired. Their four children were grown and living away from home, but a granddaughter soon visited and befriended Muriel. Muriel and Fred settled into life in a house where "we had a maid, the standard of living much higher. The house we lived in was large and spacious. We had two homes, one a weekend cottage by the lake." Fred noticed "the modern lighting system and all electrical appliances."

Tony and Geoff found themselves in similar circumstances. Their foster parents owned a music company, and they had "servants, cars, a large home in Winnipeg and a summer house in Lac du Bonnet." Mr. Ross was advanced in years and rather startled when his wife came home with two young boys in tow. Mrs. Ross herself was "elderly" and it was her daughter, Margo, "who took the part of the stern parent" and would be the one who raised the boys: "My parents had asked for two children as they were afraid one child would be lonely in a family of adults." The boys called her Margo and their foster parents Auntie and Uncle. Only Hazel called her foster parents "Mr." and "Mrs."

Hazel felt bewildered in her new home: "Sometimes I felt that we were 'show pieces' when introduced to relatives and friends of foster parents." She had difficulty establishing a connection with her family at first and she felt lonely and concerned about her brothers and sisters now scattered across town. They phoned each other and the three sets of foster parents arranged occasional visits. "Tony and Geoff were just a couple of miles away, and we often walked or cycled to see one another. My brother Fred and sister Muriel were with a family nearer the city center—hence a bus ride was necessary to visit. Their family had a car as did the twins' family so they often brought us together." Hazel found these visits reassuring and, at first, the children saw each other about once a month.

Most of the children the Curtises met were curious and friendly— "fascinated by our accents" — and ready to accept the guest children. Hazel found that "the odd one or two called us 'Bomb Dodgers' but it didn't really bother us." Nine-year-old Fred was sometimes called a coward and had "schoolboy type fights occasionally," but they all found it easy to make friends in their neighborhoods and schools. Margo Ross thought the twins "were happy well-adjusted children. No discipline problems, only the normal mischief of small boys. I think our neighbors went out of their way to make them feel at home. The boys fitted into our family perfectly. The older members became aunts and uncles and our nieces and nephews cousins."

Hazel thought school "marvelous. I was able to go to high school without passing exams or getting a scholarship. Everyone had the same opportunity and I sure took advantage of it. The coeducation was a bit of a shock after separate schooling, but I soon learned to accept the situation. The teachers were very tolerant when it came to 'money maths' and History. I had only touched on Canadian history so had a lot to learn. They were very willing to spend extra half-hours to help me after school." All the children thought their teachers kind, tolerant and helpful, which was especially important for the four younger ones. The twins had started school before leaving home, but Geoffrey found it difficult "adjusting to the school system." Fred "felt rather lost to begin with" in his large school and had "difficulties as I was two years behind in learning." The special care their teachers took with them helped them to enjoy their time in school. Tony remains sure that educational opportunities were much greater for him in Canada than in England, and Fred now believes "I would have achieved a higher standard of education" if he had stayed in Canada.

The guest children in Winnipeg "were treated very well. We had free books, free medical and dental." From time to time, they were reminded that they were a special group by various activities sponsored by Child Welfare. There were visits to the theater, parties, and on one occasion, a special reception for Marjorie Maxse as she passed through town on a Canadian tour in 1944. The 125 guests were "the happiest, healthiest lot I've seen in some time" Maxse was reported as telling them. A newspaper reporter wrote that "the British children looked more Canadian than Old Country. Only Geoffrey and Anthony Curtis had knee pants and blazers. 'But they're dying to wear longs'," Mrs. Ross confided. The twins were eager to become Canadians, and they came to feel completely at home in their five years in Winnipeg. "We became Canadian, absorbed into the Ross family, and completely assimilated," Tony recalls. The large Ross clan gave them security and defined their world. Muriel, on the other hand, "always felt foreign" during her time in Canada. Hazel "did start to think as a Canadian. I felt I had to, to be accepted by everyone. Canadians were very proud of what they were doing and didn't want me to always be talking of the ways we did it back home." At heart, however, Hazel always felt that she was English.

During the four years that Hazel was in Winnipeg, the children began to grow apart despite her efforts to keep them together. Their host families moved in different circles, their own interests changed

154

and the age gap seemed to widen. Maintaining the regular visits grew more and more difficult, and "we didn't see each other as often as we should have" Tony remembers. Each year, Tony and Geoffrey spent the months from June to September at the summer house on Lac du Bonnet—without their brother and sisters. Hazel alone could not hold them together.

In the summer of 1944 Hazel had to make a choice. "I had passed my Grade XI and could have gone on to College, but my mother was sick . . . it was felt that I should return home rather than start something I might not finish. Had I stayed on, I might have got too involved." In June 1944 she left for home. The younger children stayed in Winnipeg until the end of the war in Europe. Two weeks after VE Day, they returned home. In Toronto and Montreal, Ross relatives met the train to say goodbye to the twins, and one uncle "found out the ship they were on and went out by launch . . . to wish them 'Bon Voyage'."

JOHN JARVIS: Age 5
CORB Evacuee

"Early days in Grimsby are memories of the peach farm, primary school. Mrs. Foster's home on Ontario Street, nasty-tasting Scott's Emulsion (a sort of cod-liver-oil potion that I've not come across anywhere else—and certainly have no great desire to look it up) a handful of sultanas to eat on the way to school, lots of fun, friends, wiener roasts on the beach at Grimsby, rabbits, hollyhocks and jumping in the piles of swept-up maple leaves." The Jarvises discovered that they

155

could not send money to help Mrs. Foster with the boys, but they managed to find a way around the regulations by paying the insurance premium on a Canadian friend's policy in England and having her give the equivalent sum to Mrs. Foster. In 1941, the British government clamped down on such arrangements, and the Jarvises found themselves unable to repeat the payments. The only help they could offer was to knit and make clothes for the boys, and Mrs. Jarvis looked for a job to help pay for their outfits. Mr. Jarvis objected to his wife working, however, and it was early 1942 before she overcame his resistance and went to work as a typist.

As the first winter approached, John enjoyed life at school. He learned how to skate, and Mrs. Foster outfitted him in "riding breeches, and windbreaker jacket, leather helmet and gloves." The early weeks were "new and exciting" but John showed few signs of homesickness. The worker from the Children's Aid Society at St. Catharines called every couple of weeks "to see the children are well and happy and also to see that the people are not put to too much expense." These visits continued throughout John's stay in Grimsby and he recalls "the occasional time when I was told to be home by a particular time and I was introduced to some visitors in the parlor who would chat to me and ask me how I was in private. At that time it just seemed to be an interruption to being out playing."

Christmas in Grimsby was a thrill for the boys. Michael was "allowed to choose the tree and of course chose the biggest, which just touched the ceiling! They had such a wonderful lot of presents. Heaps of games and such things as sleighs, toboggans, books, aeroplane, submarine, knives and skates." One Christmas "the local cinema owner gave me a roll of tickets so I could go to the Saturday matinee." His foster mother took charge of them and "gave me one each Saturday or else I would have bribed the whole school with them."

John settled down happily in Grimsby, and the photos sent home convinced Mrs. Jarvis that the boys were eating well and were content with Mrs. Foster. "I am glad the boys do not get homesick," Mrs. Jarvis wrote, "I did used to worry about John as I said he was so affectionate and quite a Mummie's boy, but school will have altered that as it would have done here." Time did not make the separation any easier for her, and as spring came she missed "taking them on the beach and for walks, there seems nothing on earth to do these days."

Mrs. Jarvis had always worried about Michael, whom she thought less openly affectionate and more "willful" than John. Her friend, Agnes, gave her the impression that he was carrying on in his old ways in Grimsby, and Mrs. Jarvis wrote to him often urging him to behave. She also asked Agnes to visit Mrs. Foster's and "have a 'motherly' talk to Michael and impress him that he is now getting quite grown-up and could best repay everyone's kindness by being good and helpful" and restraining the "bit of the devil in him." The letters and talks had little effect. This proved to be a problem when Mrs. Foster sold her farm and moved into an apartment in Grimsby with the two boys. No longer young, she found that life in an apartment on Depot Street with two rowdy children was more than she could handle. John was no longer as dependent on his brother as he had been when they arrived. "I only have pleasant memories of everything but I understand that as she and we got older, my brother and I squabbled a lot . . . so Michael went to live on another farm a few miles away, and I went across the road and up Depot Street about fifty yards" to a new family.

The family John joined were also called Jarvis. The parents had come from England, and there were six children in the family—three boys who were in the services, and three girls, the youngest of whom was five years older than John. The Jarvises owned a bakery and "had shops in Grimsby, St. Catharines and Hamilton and delivered bread to all points between." They were active churchgoers and sang in the local church choir. "We had a church next door, but Mr. Jarvis insisted that, as I was from England, I should go to the Anglican church the other side of town— and sing in the choir, too. He would come and sing in the choir there, too, as well as attend other churches. I think he would have sung in anyone's choir for the sheer joy of singing.

"It wasn't really a foster home. I was adopted by the family and felt wholly part of it. The family absorbed me and probably spoilt me." John enjoyed the bustle of "a large family coming and going all the time." His foster sisters took to him naturally although the youngest one remembers being "a little jealous as I was the youngest of six and the rest were much older, so I had to share this little brother with my mother." When he arrived at the Jarvises he was wearing "short gray pants, blue blazer and cap, so he seemed very British" but he fitted in easily and "was very much one of us." Sometimes Mr. Jarvis would take him in the car to "visit the shops in far-off Hamilton and St. Catharines (it seemed very far to me). Mrs. Jarvis was the mother image and I never doubted her love and affection for us all. The next three years until I returned to England were, I suppose, a boy's golden childhood."

John enjoyed school, and developed a pride in being Canadian "when we raised the flag and sang 'Oh Canada'." His memories of Southport dimmed and his parents' images faded. "I knew I had parents in England but it all seemed pretty remote, I guess like having a favorite Uncle and Aunt that you wrote to and received presents from." Closer to home, "I still saw quite a bit of my brother at school and when he went to High School he would sometimes come over and say hello but I guess we must have drifted apart a bit. I had all my friends about me and my Canadian family." He was shocked to be told just before his tenth birthday that it was time for him to go back home.

BETTY HEELEY: Age 9
Rotary Evacuee

There were many guest children in Windsor in 1940, and Betty had no trouble gaining the acceptance of the Canadian children. Most "accepted me at once. They were very interested and seemed able to grasp my feelings at leaving my family without actually discussing it." At first, the children found her accent odd and they thought she spoke too quickly; but after a few months, that began to change. In a short time, she spoke just like her classmates did at Hugh Beaton school.

The foster families made a special effort to keep Betty and her brother Michael in touch. They met every week at the church to which both families belonged, and got together for family meals and holiday trips, including a visit to Niagara Falls before school began. Betty always found comfort in the fact that Michael was close by, and when he moved away from the neighborhood her foster parents made special efforts to drive her over for visits. After she was given a bicycle, she would often ride to Michael's, and she always telephoned him when she felt like a chat.

Betty's parents and foster parents began to write to each other as soon as she reached Windsor, and Betty kept in touch with Holmfirth through a stream of letters from home. It was Betty's father who did most of the writing, as her mother thought she was "not very much good at letter writing." In her first letter to Windsor, in October 1940, Betty's mother wrote to Auntie: "you say the time has passed quickly since Betty came to you, but it has felt a terrible long time to us. It will have felt so different for you to have a child around but isn't it grand. Our house feels terribly quiet without our children, but thank God and you good people, they are safe." Ironically, Betty's mother filled some of her empty time with volunteer work at the Holmfirth Red Cross helping with evacuees, and in November a family of evacuees came to live with them.

Betty was put into Grade 5 and found the work easy. Her father told her not to worry about that as "it is better for you to be well on top of your work." By November, Betty was growing quickly and the clothes she had brought with her from England had to be let down. Her parents could not send money, but

160

her grandmother spent much of her time sewing and knitting, since there were few restrictions on sending clothes to Canada. Betty was used to having her clothes made at home and found it quite surprising when Mrs. Hardy first took her to a shop to buy clothes. Betty was not quite so pleased with some of the clothes parcels from Holmfirth — especially the long stockings her family assumed she needed to withstand cold Canadian winters.

By November 1940, Betty's father was growing more exasperated with her long silences. A month before Christmas, he wrote: "I wonder when I shall be able to start my letter to you 'many thanks for your letter of etc.' . . . The two letters you did manage to write were very nice." Betty improved a little after that, although her older brother wrote more often. The young girl found it difficult to write a letter that would please Mrs. Hardy. "Edith wanted big letters and she read them — not to censor them but for grammar and so on. I was afraid of criticism and so I didn't write at all. . . . I couldn't explain to Edith or my parents."

There were plenty of things to write about, however. Betty developed a habit of asking for clothes, toys and other gifts. She wanted a Baby Wettums doll, a pram, special frocks and her foster parents often gave them to her. The Heeleys warned her not to keep asking for presents, and Mrs. Heeley wrote to Edith to tell her to be firm: "I know she has a way of getting round you, she was the same with her Daddy. Tell her it is her share towards helping to win the war to do without things." The Hardys, like many parents of only children, tended to overindulge Betty on some occasions and to be strict on others. Edith consulted a mother next door who had a daughter a year younger than Betty about bedtime and other discipline questions. Betty remembers her own indignation at being put on the same schedule "as someone a year younger than me."

The news from home in the spring of 1941 was full of changes. Her parents let their house and the family scattered. Betty's father, at 40 years of age, went off to the Royal Naval College on a course as a Sub-Lieutenant in the RNVR and was then posted to Liverpool, where his wife joined him in lodgings. Betty grew upset by the moves, finding it hard to picture her parents without "the base" of familiar surroundings. In time, they seemed to fade a little in her memory. Now it was Mr. Heeley's turn to apologize for long delays between letters. In the summer of 1941, when Betty and Michael were taken to Port Arthur for a holiday, their parents realized once again how different the experiences of their children were to their own. A year after the children had sailed, their father wrote: "We can hardly think what a 1,000-mile trip is like, especially when we used to think going to London (200) a long way. You certainly have seen a lot of things your Mummy and Daddy will never be able to see. . . . I guess you talk with a Canadian accent by now. . . . We often look at the Princes' landing stage where you boarded the steamer and think about your going and wish that the war would soon end, so that we could meet you coming back. You are both having such a good time that you may not want to come home when the war finishes." Betty's father began to meet Canadian troops as they disembarked and ask "Anyone here from Windsor?" He would talk to the men about the town where his children were living, and sometimes a returning sailor would drop by the foster homes with a message from England.

Betty began piano lessons and even started writing home more regularly. She worried about how her relatives were coping with wartime shortages, even though her grandmother told her at Christmastime in 1941 that she was getting enough to eat and "doing very well, really, we don't get a big variety but we are doing all right. We don't get much fruit, but we just have to do without it." It was hard for Betty to "imagine the quantities of food they had. I tried to understand by measuring the butter but I couldn't grasp that that wasn't just for table but was for cooking too. I didn't understand how anyone could tell you how much food you could buy." Her parents shared in the stages of her life from a distance, sending her a confirmation present and applauding her successes in piano exams and recitals. "We shall look forward to your entertaining us with songs at the piano when you come back home." Betty reminded her father that he had once said he would buy her a baby grand if she learned to play, but Mr. Heeley claimed not to remember his rash promise.

In Betty's second year in Canada she learned that she had a new brother, Timothy. Her father sent her a photograph of the baby and added, "The old gentleman holding Tim is your Daddy. Mummy says I look much older on photographs." Mr. Heeley had been invalided out of the RNVR with stomach ulcers and had returned to Holmfirth. Betty "wasn't told that he was ill, only that he was home." Betty might have been upset by the news of a brother born while she was away but instead was delighted, and promptly sent her younger brother a letter welcoming him into the family. The baby's antics filled her grandmother's letters. In one she told Betty that her brother was now saying "Dad dad dad and mam mam mam . . . you remember your picture you had taken in your pram, the colored one, when you were a baby. Well we have it on the wall, by the fire in my room, and when I am nursing him I tell him where his little sister Betty is, and he looks up at your picture and laughs." Betty was fascinated by the descriptions of her brother's toys — tin cans and wooden toys. All her own toys were bought at the store and "I realized they had to make Timothy's toys. We didn't have wooden toys." That summer the hit song in Canada and England was the "White Cliffs of Dover" and the family substituted Timmy for Jimmy when they sang the lyrics. It made Betty happy to think that her parents and her grandmother were all together again in their old house and that, with the addition of Timmy, things at home were as they had been when she left in 1940.

FRED: Age 13
CORB Evacuee

The combination of a homesick city boy and his resentful, hard-pressed farmer uncle was bound to result in unhappiness all around. Fred's uncle regarded the boy as an expense: "I was informed in an indirect way by my uncle saying that he was getting next to nothing for my keep and that I was going to have to work for it — and believe me I did. Because of the war labor was scarce. I was fairly big for my age, so he didn't see me as a schoolboy but as an extra hand for the farm." Most city boys would have found the routine of farm children demanding, but Fred's uncle demanded more of him than was usual, even on the farm. Although his uncle complained that Fred was lazy and did not do enough work, the Child Welfare agencies heard reports that he expected too much of the boy. After he had been on the farm for a year, Fred was questioned about his persistent lateness at school. Inquiries showed that he was late because of the number of chores he had to finish each morning. Worse, he had to spend many nights attending to the fires in the greenhouses.

His foster parents thought Fred stubborn, lazy and disobedient as he resisted the heavy demands they made on him. They had experience with their own five children and probably regarded what they asked as reasonable, but in their demands there was an undertone of resentment against the brother who had so casually lumbered them with a new child after their own family was grown. When Child Welfare suggested that Fred should go to Winnipeg for his Grade XII his foster father rejected the idea because of the expense. Fred would carry on at the village school.

The village school was an escape from his home life. "I was treated with some amusement at first because of the different accent and the wearing of short trousers, but that was for a very short period and it wasn't long before we were completely integrated. I was soon included in all aspects of the village life." Fred had been a scholarship boy at his local grammar school and had finished two years there before he came to Canada. "This allowed me into Grade XI at thirteen years of age. The next youngest in Grade XI was sixteen years of age so all my classmates were like grown men and women. In consequence, the teacher-pupil relationship was much more relaxed than I'd been accustomed to. In the U.K. High School, all the masters wore their university caps and gowns. And being so young I was looked upon as a 'boy genius.' This wasn't good for me — I was miles ahead of that Grade XI in Maths and the Sciences — but not so good in other subjects."

During his second year in Manitoba, however, he began to lose interest in school work and to think instead of ways of escaping from his uncle's farm. The choice was work or the armed services. Fred talked to the social worker about his future and told her he preferred work to school but would really like to join one of Britain's armed forces. For a while he talked of joining the RAF as a boy entrant but gave up that idea. Early in 1942, he tried to find out how he could become a mechanic but learned that he was still too young to be admitted to Vocational School. He talked instead of joining the Royal Navy. It was a big step and Fred was not sure about taking it, especially because it meant leaving his brother, whom he saw "very regularly" at his uncle's home. That home was a happier one, and Fred enjoyed his visits there. All through the early months of 1942, Fred wrestled with the idea of joining the Royal Navy. His parents preferred the RAF, but were prepared to let him join the Navy. By the summer of 1942, his father regretted his decision to send the boys to Canada. He wrote "it would I think have been better if I had kept them at home and let them take their chance. The schoolboy friends of the boys who stayed seem to have come off best. Their scholarships took them through High School to the Higher School Certificate . . . of course things may get worse [and] then we will perhaps be glad the boys are away."

For Fred, things were getting worse in Canada. That summer, he took steps to enlist. The Royal Navy required his parents to sign the forms before he could be taken on as a boy entrant, and he sent them off to England. Fred and his uncle grew increasingly irritated with one another during the hectic summer season of 1942. One morning there was an explosion. "I remember loading his truck for market at about six o'clock in the morning and then gathering together my very few possessions and setting off down the road to the village and my other uncle's house. I joined a mobile threshing gang for a few weeks and I slept at my Uncle's house. . . . when the harvest was completed, I moved onto a fox ranch — I dined in the rancher's house and slept in the bunkhouse. The work entailed killing and pelting Silver Fox and mink. During this period, I didn't see anyone from CORB, but I know the uncle I'd left communicated with them." It was a couple of months before Child Welfare caught up with Fred, but when the social worker called, she found his work and wages satisfactory and Fred glad to be away from his uncle's farm.

Child Welfare was less happy with Fred's next move, although it suited him quite well. "When the pelting season had finished, I moved on into Winnipeg and started work at the Standard Machine Works servicing Jacobs engines for Avro Anson aircraft." Fred was on "permanent night shift in the aircraft factory and earning worthwhile money" and was lodging with a couple whose son also worked at the factory. "I was fed satisfactorily and had a clean bed and I saw no problem." He was happy with his job, his home and his friends in Winnipeg.

The Child Welfare agency did see a problem, however, and the social worker called on Fred again. The department thought his lodgings were unsuitable because the family was Roman Catholic and the couple were unmarried. The social worker "told me I was in Canada under their auspices and that they didn't approve of the residence I was lodging in" and should find another place. The Department had no success in finding new lodgings and the social worker told Fred "that I either had to return to my Uncle on the farm or to fill in the forms she had with her for the Royal Navy—I can't remember being offered the possibility of going into a children's home or institution." The Department was following up on Fred's earlier interest in the Navy, but now he felt he was being pushed into a decision he was not sure about. Once he agreed in January 1943, "it all happened very quickly from that point. Within two or three weeks I'd had a medical and was on my way." Fred left Winnipeg in February 1943, and headed back to Halifax, where he had landed two-and-a-half years before, to report to HMCS *Cornwallis*. "The ironic thing was that when I arrived at the Naval base the officers and Chief Petty officers who I came into contact with did everything in their power to dissuade me from joining the RN as a Boy seaman. Most of them were RN seconded to the RCN for the period of hostilities."

GRANIA O'BRIEN: Age 12
Lady Eden's School

Chaudière House was a self-contained community. Grania was soon hard at work helping to run the school since Lady Eden had little money for staff. For a year, when she was about fourteen, Grania "only attended a few school classes" and spent the rest of her time cooking for the other children. "The older girls became teachers when they turned seventeen or eighteen" and Grania's own sister left to attend school in Montreal until she was old enough to go back to Britain and join the Wrens. Deirdre did come back to Chaudière House for the school holidays and Grania remained in close touch with her for as long as she was in Canada.

Grania got to know members of the sponsoring Breakey families and became friendly with some of the younger Breakeys; but the conditions under which she lived — cooking in the kitchen in her second-hand clothes passed on to the school from concerned Canadians — left her "aware of how it feels to live on charity." When her parents were allowed to start sending money to Canada in 1942, it "went into the general kitty" to keep the school going. Money was always short and children steadily drifted away from Lady Eden's commune-like school as their parents made new arrangements or found a way of getting them back to Britain.

The school's neighbors "were wonderful and couldn't do enough for us. In the winter, they flooded a barn so we could skate, provided sleighs and a slide for the sleighs. At Christmas, they gave us parties and very generous presents. In the summer, they arranged safe swimming places in the river." One thing missing from this world, however, was any real contact with Canadian children. "Regrettably, we never met Canadian children and I think the local ones thought we were rather strange. I did make friends with a young French Canadian girl who helped in the house at one time, and kept up a correspondence with her for a short time when I left Canada." The result was a strangely ambivalent feeling. "We always felt foreign, I suppose because we were an island to ourselves. I was, on the other hand, very proud to have a Canadian passport (I travelled out on my sister's and had to get one when she left) and tried to keep it when I went home. Not really from swank but from the fact that Canada had been my home during my formative years. So perhaps in a sense I did begin to feel slightly Canadian."

The news from home was news of change. Grania's father was granted permanent leave from the army to farm. As the threat of invasion receded, her parents moved to Ireland to open up the family house and prepare to make it home for the family. It upset Grania because "we hadn't lived in Ireland so even [with] my home there was no point of contact." Letters came regularly, but the longer Grania spent in Canada the more trouble she had remembering her parents and "how they looked and reacted. After three years, all I had in common with them was my dog who stayed behind."

In 1940, Grania had been given no choice about going to Canada; in 1943, she had no choice about going home. Early in 1943, Lady Eden decided to abandon her efforts to keep the school open and prepared to return to Britain. She booked passages for those children who wanted to go back. Mr. and Mrs. O'Brien did not want Grania to come home before the end of the war, but they were unable to find a family in Canada or the U.S.A. to foster their daughter. While her parents searched for a family, Grania learned that her passage was available. The efforts to find her a new home were abandoned, and in May 1943, she left Breakeyville.

HAZEL WILSON: Age 14
CORB Evacuee

It took Hazel a long time to overcome her sense of loneliness and insecurity after arriving in Canada. Her brother lived eight miles away and was rarely able to cycle over to see her. Hazel phoned him from time to time, and over the years "spent a lot of time with my brother's friends." In her first months in Winnipeg she "felt under a lot of pressure and lonely. I was afraid that if I caused problems it would upset my parents back home whom I figured were having a bad time worrying about us anyway." She had to make her own efforts to adjust to new ways of doing things at home, and to the life at Linwood Collegiate.

There were compensations. "Food was the biggest change. I had never seen so much beautiful food in my life. We grew all our own veg in England, but ate very plainly. Cakes and ice cream, pumpkin pies— now all treats. I grew five inches the first year. My brother grew eleven inches." Her foster mother was "a fantastic cook" and, more importantly, she was "devoted" to Hazel and helped her cope with the loneliness and insecurity. They shared a sense of humor, although Hazel's world was more one of private jokes. "I always had humorous thoughts and enjoyed them but didn't think anyone else would. I later found out I was wrong." Mrs. Rook "taught me I could do anything I set my mind to." The Rooks plunged Hazel into their world of music. She learned to play the piano and joined her foster parents in St. Andrew's Oak Street church choir, where Hazel fell in love with the organist. The Rooks' neighbors made a fuss of Hazel, but she found it difficult at first to make friends her own age. She joined the Girl Guides and spent her summers at Guide camp and working on farms in Manitoba. Gradually, her circle of friends grew from Church activities and the Guides.

Hazel had "always hated school from eleven years on" and at Linwood Collegiate she was put into "Grade 11 which was matric in Manitoba . . . everyone was much older than I." The children treated her with curiosity: "She's the only girl in school with straight hair!" Hazel felt awkward among these apparently self-assured young people, and she found it a shock to be in a mixed school after the all-girls Greyfriars school she had attended in Colchester. "The class consisted of five girls and twenty-one boys — pretty heavy, especially after an all-girls school." The clothes she was given that first winter added to her embarrassment. Her winter outfit came from the Red Cross. "The coat I got had a fox collar and was made of herringbone tweed, circa 1930. Can you imagine a teenager being dressed like that? I used to hide in the cloakroom at school. Don't even mention *black oxfords!* As painful as this was, I never uttered a word because I felt everyone was being so kind in their way." As soon as she could, Hazel left school and enrolled at the Angus School of Commerce, which gave her, as a guest child, a year's free instruction. Despite her unhappy time at school Hazel is "absolutely" certain that she had a better education in Canada than she would have had in wartime Britain, and she remains convinced that it opened opportunities for her she would not have had at home. In November 1943, Hazel began work at the Manitoba Liquor Commission and enjoyed the independence of being out of school and earning money. Her circle of friends widened further and she became more confident.

Hazel thought often of home and was glad to hear from her parents about Colchester and her little sister. She never felt that she was losing touch and on June 6, 1944, noted in her diary: "Hurrah, the invasion started today. Will be home sooner, I hope." She was approaching the age when CORB sent children home, and on the last day of June, she and her brother went to the Children's Aid Society where the social worker told us "we could go home." Hazel "felt great — very excited. Looking forward to seeing a sister who was two years old when we left [and] also our loving parents." There was no further word about leaving for home in July, but in August, CORB confirmed the decision and Hazel began a round of goodbyes. Forty Woodhaven people gave her a pen and pencil set, a photo album and some nail polish. The Rooks gave her a watch and her fellow workers gave her a necklace and locket. The "biggest thrill was being presented with a Canadian passport" early in September. She left for home the following month.

CYNTHIA LORD: Age 11
St. Hilda's School (Alma College)

Cynthia remembers her years in St. Thomas as "the happiest time of my life." She plunged into life at Alma College where "there were lots of Americans and girls from South America, too; we weren't the only ones who were on our own." The St. Hilda's girls were assigned to a separate house for their first year at the request of Sister Elsa, who still hoped to find a school big enough to hold all her 160 pupils. Cynthia and most of her friends at Alma, however, felt little loyalty to St. Hilda's. "When the nuns finally found a school large enough for us all I am afraid most of the Alma contingent refused to go back to St. Hilda's, and so we spent all the four years at the same school." When she learned of the plans to reunite St. Hilda's, Cynthia pleaded in a letter home, "Mummy darling do I *have* to go to St. Hilda's any more (at least when I come back?)" She complained that at St. Hilda's "they *make* you have senna every Sunday. Mummy there is *no* comparison whatever between S.H. and 'dear old Alma.' I do so love Alma. S.H. is so filthy. If a sister drops a sausage on the floor she picks it up and eats it, they say you must not waste." Life at Alma was much less Spartan than in the English school. On another occasion, Cynthia said she was "going To Raise Hell" if she was sent back to St. Hilda's. Her parents agreed to let her stay and the sponsors helped to meet the costs.

Cynthia's mother sent her clothes parcels as often as she could, and Cynthia wrote often to ask for what she needed. It was hard for Mrs. Lord, in wartime Britain, to keep up with the demands of an adolescent

174

girl at a fashionable boarding school. Sometimes Cynthia "hated" the clothes she was sent. Cynthia's sponsors helped. "I think our sponsors must have bought a lot of our clothes, although we didn't have many . . . as the school allowed everyone to wear their own clothes after four o'clock . . . it was rather hard, really." Cynthia knew that Alma had made a special concession to the British school by taking the girls in for the much lower fees paid at St. Hilda's. Even those reduced fees had to be paid by sponsors and supporters of Alma until 1942. Cynthia was never clearly told about money problems but she was aware of them. "We were painfully aware that we had hardly any pocket money. The school shop was allowed to give us a small amount of credit, [but] I don't remember ever having more than enough to buy toothpaste and writing paper, and a few sweets. Some girls did better than I did."

Despite the money problems, Cynthia loved Alma. In the first year, when the St. Hilda's girls were a separate unit in the school, they were a little apart from their classmates. After that arrangement was abandoned, "we joined in the life of the school on more equal terms. The older girls tended to adopt us." There was some teasing about accents at first but no real hostility, and the teachers treated her "absolutely marvelously." Cynthia felt secure inside the school's close-knit circle. Sometimes the community was a little too close, however, and friendships were volatile. Principal P.S. Dobson had to assure the Lords that Cynthia was happy at the school: "The children do change about a little in their friendships and preferences and I think this is quite normal for them to do so. It seems that the children sometimes make remarks in letters which are just the expression of their mood at that particular moment. Then it is only natural for you, at such a great distance, to read more meaning into the remark than is really intended. I must say that Cynthia seems extremely happy and well." Cynthia herself assured her parents as the school year opened in 1942 that "I'm getting along just fine so don't any of you worry about me. Oh Mummy, it's so hard not to grow up. But I can, really I can, be your little girl again just any time you want it."

Cynthia sometimes felt a distance opening between herself and her family in England, despite the weekly letters she wrote home and the frequent letters she sent to her older brother. Often, as the war went on, Cynthia wrote to urge her parents to come to Canada to settle once the war was over. She assured them that if they came to Alma and St. Thomas, they would love them as much as she did herself. When plans for going home were in the air, Cynthia wrote: "you know, I mean to come back to Canada sometime. I will be awfully homesick for it. Its beauty can't compare with England, but other things can." Despite her growing affection for Canada, however, she never felt Canadian: "I always thought of myself as English."

Cynthia spent vacations from the school at the homes of schoolfriends or with Helen at their sponsors' home in Cobourg. The girls "did love our sponsors" but sometimes the long summers in Cobourg were difficult. Dr. Dobson wrote to the Lords that Cynthia and Helen were sometimes too much in each others' company and consequently quarreled and bickered. The bickering had other roots, too, for at times Cynthia felt more like a guest than a family member in her sponsors' home. Reflecting on the summers at Cobourg in 1944, Cynthia wrote: "I want to feel as if I *own* a home again where I can walk in the front door and yell like anything 'Hello Mummy and Daddy.' I feel as if I'm lost. I can't walk into Cobourg and feel as if *I* own it like I do at home. I want the war to be over, so Jackie can sit in one armchair again and me on the floor. I remember how he used to pester me to get him another apple, orange, etc."

In the later years of the war, Cynthia spent some of her summer vacation working on the fruit farms around St. Thomas. She spent her days off with the gang at the beach or the local dance hall and ice-cream parlor, and it was there that Cynthia saw a strange machine she described to her parents. "It was a gramophone affair much bigger than a radio and it lights up. You press a button and choose your record, press its number and put a nickle in it. Mr. Burns (Jane's friend) paid for 20 and more records." Despite the fun on rare days off, Cynthia hated farm work — strawberries were gooey and she was afraid of falling off the ladder when the wind blew through the cherry trees. She was glad enough to spend time at Cobourg after a spell on the farm or to escape to a friend's home before returning to school. It was after a weekend with a family in Tillsonburg that Cynthia returned to school late in May 1944 to learn that plans were under way for her to go back to Britain. "I hated to go home. I had a very nice boyfriend that I still keep in touch with, and I would have been quite happy to stay and finish my education."

CHAPTER VII

❖

FOR
THE DURATION

❖

A S the years in Canada succeeded one another, guest children lived under the peculiar strain of knowing that the connection with their Canadian family would be broken arbitrarily at some time in the future. Many of the foster parents felt that they had to remind the children that the arrangement was temporary. Younger children found this difficult to understand. One foster mother, who cared for a two-year-old boy and his older sister, found that "I had difficulty explaining to him that I was not his mother — he ended up always with 'but you're just like my mummy aren't you?'" His own mother refused to allow him to call his foster mother by any name that suggested she was his mother. However hard foster parents worked to keep the children in touch with home, the links often weakened as memories faded. A young boy told his foster mother as he left home in

1943, "Don't put anyone in my bed for I will be back very soon."[1]

There were few ways of keeping the memories of home fresh. The cable companies allowed each guest child to cable a free message monthly from a prepared list and many children used this service. CORB arranged for photos of the children to be sent home soon after they were settled and received many letters of thanks for such efforts. Parents depended heavily on letters and snapshots, but many children found it difficult to write a weekly letter or to know what to put in it. Many letters were lost on voyages across the Atlantic, and some people began to number each letter so that their correspondents would know if one had gone down. In the style of all family correspondence, letters to the guest children tended to open with requests for longer and more frequent letters. Parents often found themselves at a similar loss for words, however, especially since many tried to shield their children from the war. As one mother explained, "Sometimes when we have not had a letter for a bit, it is quite a problem to find something to say in our weekly letter as we do not mention the war much." This disturbed children who were anxious to know how the war was affecting their families. If there was a long silence from home, the children began to worry that something had happened to their parents.

Even for parents who managed to write regularly, the letters themselves could illustrate the growing distance between the family members. A social worker noted that one young man's letters were still addressed to him as "Master" — even when he was about to leave school and enter the forces. Some parents caused tension between their children by addressing all the letters and parcels to one child or by sending presents to one child but not to the others. The net result was often squabbling among the children or depression in the child who felt neglected. Children who heard nothing from home were especially unhappy and some developed serious emotional problems. Silence from home intensified one girl's anxiety and was partly responsible for her developing ulcers. A boy who did not hear from his mother for three months became "restless and difficult." Another boy, who had no word from home for three years, had to be referred to a Child Guidance Clinic where the psychologist reported that the boy had suffered from a "feeling of rejection for a long time" and now felt that he did not want anyone to take an interest in him.[2]

Some of the most sustained correspondence travelled between parents and foster parents. Adult to adult, they talked of the war, of rationing, of the stress of daily life and of their feelings about the separation. A mother wrote in 1942, "Fancy, they will have been away for two years in August, seems a lifetime, how I had planned their little lives and to enjoy their company and love . . . little did I think someone else would be bringing them up in the best years of their life. Sometimes I wonder if it was worthwhile having children, just to part with them and live in unhappiness for years. . . . If I could get over now, nothing would stop me, that's how I feel but I know there is no hope so must keep on and work hard and forget."

In an attempt to close the gap between parents and children, CORB turned to radio. Broadcasts by the guest children and their parents began in 1940. At first these were recorded messages, but they were soon replaced by direct shortwave transmissions, and even by two-way conversations between parents and children. The broadcasts required elaborate preparation and could be a strain on those taking part. As one parent explained in a letter to her children's foster parents, "We put our names down in January and were asked to go to Manchester last Saturday and make a recording. I was terribly nervous and rather mixed up my message but I don't think it will sound so bad. It was rather an ordeal as you had to speak your message into the microphone before all the room full of parents (30). Fortunately we waited till next to last. Even then, I was nervous but did not break into tears like one or two poor souls did; it was a pity they did not retake them as I think it would be most upsetting to the children to hear their mothers almost in tears . . . after saying the lines through umpteen times and having to get the whole message including addresses in 30 seconds, the message seems quite meaningless to us." The BBC could not tell them when the record would be played on the Canadian children's hour and it was impossible to let the children know when to listen.

The two-way exchanges were even more emotional. A reporter from the *Yorkshire Post* was present in the studio at Leeds on Christmas Day, 1940, when parents and children took part in a hookup with Canada and the United States called "Children Calling Home." The parents stood around a hanging microphone with their written messages in their hands "tense and quietly excited." When the conversations began, some of the parents learned how quickly their children were becoming Canadian. Seven-year-old John was bewildered by questions about Father Christmas until the Canadian announcer translated that into Santa Claus. Most of the parents' questions brought brief "OKs" and "Sures" in response. The BBC began to caution parents against commenting on the children's accents, since it often upset them. Listening to the broadcast on Christmas day, one mother thought "the children all sounded very happy if a little bewildered. The parents did very well though one or two of them seemed a little full up hearing their dear voices."

Most of the broadcasts were over the shortwave, and after 1940, the children were sent a cable announcing the date of the broadcast. Not everyone had a shortwave radio but few could wait until the messages were rebroadcast by CBC. The cable, therefore, produced a flurry of activity as families searched for neighbors with the right kind of radio. In Manitoba, Duncan's family piled into the horse-drawn cutter when the cable came and drove to a neighbor's home to hear his mother's broadcast. A bewildered Duncan reported, "it didn't sound like Mum at all. Of course, I guess she was speaking English, like we had to at school. She never talked to me like that at home." Duncan was not the only guest child who heard his parents, under the strain of speaking in a room full of strangers, put on a "posh" voice. The broadcasts brought mixed emotions and often upset the children. Dudley was left wondering "if he would ever see them again" after hearing his parents, and Jean was very upset after she had spoken on the radio. Some parents did not trust their own emotions or worried about the effects of the broadcasts and refused to take part. Eight-year-old David wrote to his mother: "I would like to know why you don't want to hear me talk on the radio" but she did not answer his question.

Some children worked out their own ways of remembering home. One young girl asked her foster parents if she could have a kipper every week, just as she had had with her father back home. Four or five years of separation, however, were difficult to bridge, and most of the guest children began to lose touch with their families at home. Younger children had the greatest difficulties remembering home. Min "just forgot about belonging to my parents after a year, and my foster folk became Mummy and Daddy." Judith had been sent to Canada at the age of two, and although she wrote to her parents, "I really did not know them." Even the older children, who remembered their parents more vividly, found the memories fading over the years. While the letters, parcels and broadcasts were enough for some to feel in touch, many shared the worries of a girl who was nine when she left home: "I used to walk home from the station in my mind, and I had started to forget some of the way . . . that worried me more than anything because I felt I must be forgetting more important things."[3]

One source of tension between guest children, their foster families and their own families was money. For the first two years of the evacuation, Britain refused to ease the regulations imposed in 1940, making it impossible to send money to the foster parents. While most of the foster parents accepted the burden willingly, some were resentful and a sensitive child could be very aware that he or she was a burden to the family. Part of the resentment Marjorie Maxse noticed among some nominated families was rooted in the feeling that they had been imposed on by the children's parents. An eight-year-old girl felt that "I was a charity case. Kept out of kindness of my relatives. It hurt me very much and I actually felt abandoned financially by my parents. I felt shame . . . at living on charity." Dudley, at twelve, knew that his parents were embarrassed at being unable to send money to Canada, and he found a job at school to pay for his lunches. When the parents of private evacuees were eventually allowed to send money, the amount was limited by the British Treasury and did not cover the children's costs in Canada. The exchange controls remained so strict that many families were unable to repay the expenses until the controls were eased in 1953.

For the CORB parents, there was the added irritation of paying a weekly contribution to the Board and knowing that it was not going to the foster family. The contribution of six to nine shillings a week could be a heavy drain on a working-class family with a number of children in Canada. More than one mother went to work specifically to meet the obligation to CORB. Not until 1942, did the British Treasury feel able to allow six shillings a week to be sent to Canada for each child. In 1944, the sum was doubled, and parents could also send a limited amount of money directly to the foster family. CORB foster parents received a book of coupons to be cashed each week and many immediately began to bank the money for the children. E.H. Blois claimed late in the war that "all the children that have gone back from this Province have taken back fair sums of money or certificates as the case may be."

Such generosity upset CORB, since the British government made up the difference between what the parents could afford to contribute and the twelve shillings each child received. Mrs. D.S. Archdale, who replaced Phyllis Snow in CORB's Ottawa office, thought it "hardly seems equitable that some children should accumulate money . . . which has been provided from public funds." There was little anyone could do to force foster parents to spend the money. Not all foster families could afford to save the money, however, and some needed further help from governments. The need for subsidies reflected the economic disparities of wartime Canada. In early 1943, only four of the six hundred CORB children in Ontario received assistance. In Saskatchewan, still struggling to recover from Canada's worst depression, nearly one-quarter of the guest children were subsidized in 1943.[4]

The National Advisory Committee stopped meeting soon after the evacuation ended, and the federal Immigration Branch took over the work of supervising the CORB children. By the beginning of 1941, $90,000 a year was being spent on the CORB scheme, with most of the money going for staff and administrative costs. The funds came from an annual Parliamentary vote after the earlier efforts to raise money by public appeals were abandoned. F.C. Blair, who was responsible for the guest children, remained vigilant and cost-conscious and always kept a sharp eye on private evacuees who got close to public money. He watched the situation in Montreal with special care because Dr. Grant Fleming, who headed the Operating Committee of COS, was too generous for Blair's peace of mind. Fleming looked on his work as a return for the hospitality he had received in Britain during World War I. He believed that the evacuee families COS supported had to be encouraged to stand on their own feet, but that they should be helped at a rate "more generous . . . than that practiced in any charitable organization."

The Quebec government allowed COS to spend provincial funds on private evacuees but it expected Ottawa to reimburse the money. Dr. Jean Gregoire, the Deputy Minister of Health, argued that the war had brought the women and children to Quebec and ultimately they were a federal responsibility. Blair agonized over the situation in Montreal because of the link between COS and the CNCR. Saul Hayes, the Treasurer of COS, had been prominent in setting up the CNCR and Blair soon convinced himself that COS was "the child of CNCR" and was thus connected with "efforts to bring in . . . a considerable number of Jewish women . . . and they are now desirous of having them supported through the Montreal council." Not only was that the plan, but COS also intended to be more generous to Jewish women than to non-Jewish women.

His official in Montreal, J.M. Byers, assured Blair that there was "no reason to think that Jewish women receive more generous treatment than others" but Blair ordered an investigation of the support given to private evacuees in 1941. By December, he had identified five cases in which women had been given money by COS and the IODE. The five cases involved a total COS expenditure of $70. Byers urged Blair to end his investigation. She reminded him that "we lack definite evidence that the Montreal women are getting too much money" and while she was ready to accept that there were "a few cases of real fraud by Jewish women" she pointed out that the inquiries had led COS to believe that Immigration was "unsympathetic to the Hebrew race." With a new, Jewish, Executive Director taking over COS, Byers thought that further investigations would make a bad impression. Blair agreed to drop the investigation, and COS supported private evacuees until February 1944, with funds from Quebec. At that time, the provincial government limited its support to children in order to save money. After Blair's retirement, Ottawa agreed to reimburse Quebec for its support of evacuees since 1940.[5]

Childcare agencies were willing to pay subsidies where they were needed, since it was thought to be better all around to help a family keep a child than to move one merely in order to maintain the ideal of a free home. What's more, the longer the war went on, the harder it became to find free homes as enthusiasm waned, costs rose and the children grew older. All the childcare agencies were kept busy in 1940–1941 moving those children who weren't happy with their first home. The number varied from CORB's 11% to the University of Toronto's 25%, but all over Canada, the pattern of replacements was the same. It began with a surge in the first few months, then dropped — sometimes to as low as 5% of the children in 1942–43 — only to pick up again toward the end of the war as more of the guest children reached their teens. Even younger children were disturbed by the loss of an older brother or sister returning to Britain and grew harder to handle.

There were many reasons for asking for a child to be moved. Some foster parents found the reality of coping with the British children far removed from the expectations they had held when they phoned the CAS in June 1940. E.H. Blois noted, in the summer of 1941, that some foster families "complain that the extra burden is too much. Not financially, I understand, but the responsibility and extra care which these children have placed on the women of the household." The cause was no longer fashionable and "women get resentful." Even without a child in the home, the enthusiasm had often gone by 1941. When the University of Toronto Committee asked families who had volunteered to take a child in 1940 if they would be willing to do so in 1941, an overwhelming majority refused.

Many foster families kept their enthusiasm but were forced to ask for a child to be moved because of illness or because the family income dropped when the father joined forces. Some families found it financially impossible to raise the children even with the father at home and financial help from the government. Wartime brought with it many dislocations, and people often moved about in search of work. Some families took their foster children with them and children moved happily from British Columbia to Alberta and from Manitoba to Ontario, but more often when a foster family moved, the child was put into a new home. Sometimes children had to be moved because they could not adjust to the home in which they found themselves. One child was very unhappy in a lavish home where she was attended by servants, but settled happily in a "less elaborate" home. Dr. MacKinnon came to believe that placing a child in a home much superior to his British one made it very difficult for him to settle in Canada. There always were homes that one report described as "satisfactory within itself but which is inadequate to the needs of this particular child." Most of these mismatches showed up early, which helps to account for the high rate of replacement when the scheme began.

Foster parents had little help in coping with the tensions as children learned to live with their new families. Manitoba's experience suggested that "there appeared to be a definite relationship between the amount of supervision and the number of replacements . . . more intensive supervision would reduce the number, since the worker supervising could sense and correct many difficulties in their early stages." With an average case load of over one hundred, however, there was little hope of social workers offering intensive supervision. Dr. Karl Bernhardt, who looked after replacement for the University of Toronto Committee, reported that difficult cases took an "enormous amount of time." One case involved "25 letters, 50 phone calls and 10 interviews." Supervising bodies tried to meet CORB's request that each child be visited twice a year, but without an appeal from the foster parents, the full six months would pass between visits.

There were some children who could not settle in any home. Each move reduced the chance of success and eventually some children were placed in paid boarding homes. If the child's behavior made even a boarding home placement impossible, the final move was to an institution. Late in 1942, no guest children were in institutions in Ontario but a number were in Manitoba. CORB was disturbed by the discrepancy

and felt that Manitoba was too quick to declare children difficult and remove them from foster homes. A
number of boys were sent to the Knowles school in
Winnipeg which specialized in educating "difficult"
boys. Marjorie Maxse, on a tour of Canada in 1944,
was sorry to see Manitoba "retreat to institutionalism"
and persuaded the Department to find new homes for
two of the CORB boys at Knowles. The most expensive
solution for children who were hard to place was to
send them to boarding schools. Ontario sent only four
of its CORB children to boarding schools in 1941, but
COS in Montreal used boarding schools more freely.
The University of Toronto committee agreed that it
was unwise to appeal for funds to send guest children
to boarding schools and looked on this as a last resort.
It was not only the cost which made Canadian agencies
reluctant to put children in schools. British parents
complained that they had sent their children to live
with families and not to be placed in boarding schools.
Most childcare agencies did their best to find private
homes for even the most difficult children.[6]

From the beginning of the evacuation it had been
clear that adolescents were the most difficult to place.
Blois once said that some of the boys were "dull homely
fellows and the older and bigger they grow the less lov-
able they become . . . some of the families just cannot
stand them much longer." Foster parents and children
argued about behavior, work and friendships. Teenage
inertia overcame some evacuees, who seemed to change
overnight from charming young children to stolid young
men who could not easily be persuaded to do their chores
or attend to their schoolwork. Independent expression of
opinion quickly became sauciness to some foster parents.

Friendships caused foster parents the most concern. Teenaged boys spent their earnings on Zoot suits and joined an older crowd of fast company. Teenagers stayed out late at night, and one boy disturbed his foster parents by an association with a woman in her twenties. Another worried his family by his associations with older men. Dating caused many confrontations. A boy who brought girls back to the house while his foster parents were away got special attention from the social worker. Foster parents of teenaged girls were even more concerned. A seventeen-year-old guest child gravely worried her foster mother because she was "boy crazy and showed no discrimination." On one occasion, she came home from a dancehall with an escort whose name she did not know and laughed when she was reprimanded. She was moved to a new home where she settled down and stayed home in the evenings when her newly acquired steady boyfriend was out of town.

The fact that the children were evacuees was seen as the root of their difficulties in some extreme cases. One boy whose behavior rapidly deteriorated in his adolescence was said to suffer from "a feeling of rest-lessness and dissatisfaction, since it was necessary for him to be taken from his own home and placed among strangers . . . in general he feels himself discriminated against and seemed to be feeling something of a martyr." Foster parents and social workers faced with teenaged guest children who resisted what the adults regarded as a reasonable exercise of authority agreed that the best solution was a move to a new home or, in serious cases, a return to Britain before the teenager's behavior caused too much trouble.[7]

Childcare workers had faith in parental discipline. The few guest children who ran afoul of the law and ended up in detention were sent home. A boy of fifteen was recommended for return in 1944 because he resented his foster mother's discipline. A teenaged girl was said by her caseworker to be "not a bad girl," but in need of "a mother's firm control" and was recommended for an early return. A CAS in British Columbia asked that a sixteen-year-old be sent home in 1943 because he was difficult to manage and was making a poor adjustment to life in Canada. But in most cases, nothing could be done because there was no space on the ships to Britain. Instead, the resentful teenager was left more conscious than ever of the temporary nature of his life in Canada.

Some teenagers were eager to join the armed forces. Guest children who left Britain in their teens or close to them were more likely than the younger children to feel guilty about being in Canada. They felt that they had run away from the war and were not "doing their bit," or were enjoying privileges their English contemporaries were denied. One fourteen-year-old boy referred to a psychiatrist was said to be suffering from guilt at leaving his widowed mother in England and because he was not out of school and working as he would have been in England. Teenagers who had already begun to work in England were often unhappy about returning to school in Canada, and were quick to volunteer for the forces or to request to be sent home to serve in Britain. B.W. Heise of Ontario agreed with this attitude and recommended that boys should be sent home at seventeen-and-a-half years of age "in order that they may acclimatize themselves to war conditions in England before receiving their call at 18½."[8]

Teenagers needed their parents' permission to return home early or to join the forces. Parents, thousands of miles away, often differed with foster parents over what was best for the children. As their children became more Canadian, British parents were uncertain about what was acceptable behavior. Canadian teens led an active social life and talk of dating and news that their daughters were using makeup upset British parents. Canadians encouraged teenagers to work after school and on weekends, but many British parents were less than certain that it was a good idea for school children to take a job. On the other hand, British parents tended to have different ideas about preparing for life after school. Canadians encouraged their children to stay in school and plan for the highest level of education they could reach. A number of guest children were encouraged to think beyond high school but some, especially from working-class families, were discouraged by parents who thought that they should leave school at fourteen and learn a trade. The tension between parents and foster parents, the long correspondence as the questions were hammered out and the mixture of hope and frustration upset teenagers. They were caught between the advice offered from home and the advice offered in Canada. It emphasized the tug of loyalties between families and between countries. When a teenager chose to ignore her parents and stay in school, she was also making a choice of Canada over Britain. If she thought of going home, she thought of preparing for life in Britain. A number of teenagers left school to learn a trade and gave up the plans for higher education they would have followed if they had been Canadian.

There is no doubt that Canada offered children more opportunity for education than many would have had at home. Because high school was free in Canada, CORB children stayed in school longer than they would have in Britain or in another Dominion. Many children who would have left school at fourteen in Britain, stayed on to matriculate in Canada. F.C. Blair did not approve. He wrote to Blois, who shared his concerns, that they should "be careful not to educate a boy in such a way that he will be a misfit in the home to which he returns. I suppose foster parents are liable to want to educate and train children to fit into the circumstances of a foster home rather than into the home they left and to which they will return." Canada also offered more chances for post-secondary education than Britain or the other Dominions. Most of the forty CORB children who took further education were among those sent to Canada. They joined the private evacuees in Canadian colleges and universities, many of which were willing to charge reduced fees or defer payment until after the war. The fees were often paid by foster parents, by remittances from Britain, by childcare agencies and by the students themselves, and CORB made some grants to youths at university. But the British Treasury objected to "higher education in North America at the cost of our dollars" and insisted that any funds sent to CORB children in university would have to be limited to £10 a month.

Money was not the only barrier to higher education, however, since youths who were old enough to go to college were old enough to serve in the war.

Britain expected the evacuees to consider war service their first priority. Boys were liable for call up at the age of eighteen, and girls could be directed into war work at eighteen and called up at nineteen. The British government was prepared to allow the evacuees to meet their obligations by joining the Canadian forces, doing war work in Canada or going home to join the British forces. Educational deferments were offered to some students in Britain, and the British agreed that "really promising" youths in Canada could be considered for deferment. At first, an evacuee who wanted further education had to return to Britain at eighteen-and-a-half years of age and study there, but in 1943, that requirement was eased. The British accepted that it was difficult to begin work at a Canadian university and then return to the much different British system. They agreed that university-age men could stay in Canada to study medicine or scientific subjects and that university-age women could remain to study these subjects or Arts courses as preparation for teaching or social work. The number of deferments was to "be small" and limited to students who were "well above average in ability." At the end of the war, some evacuees were allowed to delay their return home to complete a school year or a course of education.[9]

A few of the guest children were shielded from the clash between British and Canadian education because they attended their British schools in Canada. But even though they followed British ways with British teachers and a British curriculum, it was impossible for them to remain totally isolated from Canada. St. Hilda's School, in its house in Erindale, became a part of the community during the war years. The girls at Erindale could be seen each week "walking uphill, crocodile fashion, to spend their weekly nickel at the store." Each Sunday, the girls half-filled St. Paul's church, which stood close to their school. They were welcomed by the congregation and admired for their singing. The girls introduced the custom of presenting a Nativity Play at the church, which continued to be a part of the church year after they returned to Britain in 1944. At the school, costs were kept down because the girls did much of the routine housework themselves. The Headmistress, Sister Elsa, was quoted as saying "they like to do it, and their parents believe they should do it." Only the heavy work and the cooking were done by hired help. After 1942, the Treasury eased its regulations and allowed money to be sent to support most of the schools. Life became easier for the children and the staff. A journalist visiting the school in its first week was surprised when Sister Elsa declared "we are becoming quite Canadian . . . The girls are using quite a number of Canadian expressions." The journalist quite clearly felt that she had stepped into a British enclave.

St. Hilda's operated as a British school in Canada. The girls wore their school uniforms of Lincoln green which were passed on to the younger children as the girls grew. "For five years I had no new clothes," a former St. Hilda's girl recalls, "I can't really remember minding this — it was just accepted." "School continued as it would have done in England — with English teachers and just the odd Canadian visiting staff." The school did keep to Canadian terms to make it easier for the Canadian families who took the girls in for holidays, but senior girls who took "English School

Certificate had to keep to English times for the exams and stayed on after school broke up." The girls found school much the same as in England, although Erindale and its grounds were more spacious and the cook served "fantastic chocolate pudding—we called it Ganges mud."

The choice between Britain and Canada surfaced from time to time for all the guest children. The very name "guest child" suggested a temporary state, and a Canadian foster sister recalls that "we knew they eventually would be going home." The children were reminded of their status on special occasions. In a large community they might be called together for a Christmas party or to meet a visiting British official. In February 1942, the guest children in Winnipeg were invited to a showing of *Babes on Broadway* starring Mickey Rooney. When children took part in school activities or fund-raising drives and got their names in the paper, they were identified as war guests. But many children struggled to understand where they truly belonged.

Children with British foster parents were less likely to think of themselves as Canadian. Margot, who was thirteen when she arrived in 1940, did not begin to feel Canadian until she left home to go to work. Children who lived with their mother in Canada were constantly reminded that they were only visitors. One girl who arrived with her mother at the age of thirteen recalls, "I never became Canadian and felt even more British as the war went on." For her, it was "a great relief" to leave in 1946. Younger children in Canadian homes tended to think of themselves as Canadians more readily, just as they were more willing to adopt

Canadian accents and usages. Some of the younger children began to feel Canadian in their first days at school, whereas older children were torn between feelings of pride in Britain and gratitude and love for Canada. It took years for some of the children to feel fully at home. Olive came to feel Canadian "just by acting as one of the girls." A girl who was twelve when she arrived only began to feel Canadian when she was old enough to work in Woolworths on Saturday and to pick fruit on local farms in the summer holidays. Eleven-year-old Donald in New Brunswick thought that learning to plow was the beginning of the change. When he found his way two miles to school on foot through a snowstorm "just like the natives" he felt he belonged. But some of the older children resisted the temptation to become Canadian. A thirteen-year-old girl "kept myself foreign deliberately. I felt very guilty at being safe, and well fed, when every member of my family at home was having a rough time." A number of the older children only identified with Canada when they joined the Canadian armed forces or, ironically, when they were given a Canadian passport to return to Britain. Despite their efforts, children who had tried to stay British sometimes were surprised at how Canadian they had become. More than one child could claim, like Patricia, that they "never felt Canadian until I returned home."[10]

Parents had begun to plan the return of their children almost as soon as they reached Canada. Many immediately regretted the decision to send their children away and were saddened when it became clear that it might be years before they saw them again. CORB refused requests to send children back to

Britain early in the war unless there were special reasons such as illness at home or an opportunity to start an apprenticeship. It was difficult to arrange passages on the crowded wartime ships even for children who had a hard time adjusting to life in Canada. Teenagers who wanted to join up were encouraged to join the Canadian forces rather than return to Britain as civilians.

Most of the children who returned early in the war were private evacuees. Few children were withdrawn from CORB by parents eager to arrange their passage home. The quickest return required a dangerous voyage by neutral ship from New York to Lisbon followed by a flight to London. The route was not only hazardous but also "prohibitively expensive." There were reports of fares as high as $850 being charged for the passage to Lisbon. Direct passages to England were available, but space was so limited that some women waited two years for a passage home. As the war went on private evacuees grew eager to go, and by late 1943, Betti Sandiford found that there was a growing feeling among Canadians that the "mothers should return home." However, it was easier to send boys home than it was to send women and girls. Boys could sign on as cadets in Merchant Navy ships sailing from New York. In 1943, the Royal Navy began a scheme that allowed boys between eight and sixteen to go home as crew on White Ensign ships. In Toronto, the arrangements were made by CPR and Cook's and were "very hush hush." To meet the demand for passages home, the British Admiralty chartered a ship in May 1944 to carry the old, mothers with children and girls under seventeen years of age. The University of Toronto committee was given some spaces on the ship and had just over a week to prepare a party of thirty-eight women and girls for the journey home. President and Mrs. Cody went down to Union Station to say goodbye to the guests. Mrs. Cody described a scene in which the "whole concourse was filled with children and pigtails flew in all directions." Although the newspapers wanted to be there to take goodbye pictures, they were barred for security reasons. The children left for home without the publicity that had greeted their arrival.

As the privately evacuated women and children found their way back to Britain in 1943 and 1944, new complaints arose about privilege. CORB and the Immigration Branch fielded more and more questions from parents who wanted their children home. A.L. Jolliffe, who had replaced Blair as Director of Immigration, admitted that "it is difficult to explain to these parents what appears to be unfair discrimination between the privately evacuated children and their own evacuated under the Government scheme." CORB children who came from parts of Britain that were less "vulnerable" to air raids left for home in November 1944. More were sent home early in 1945 as the war in Europe drew to its close.[11]

The news that they were going home brought out the same mixed emotions the children had felt in 1940. The older children were the first to leave, which left their younger brothers and sisters upset and worried about going home alone. Guest children who were going home to changed circumstances were especially anxious about the move. A girl who had spent the war at St. Hilda's found her return home at the age of seventeen, "much more disruptive than when I came," although she was pleased to be going. She had to face the fact that her parents had divorced while she was in Canada, and she worried whether either parent "would be able to offer me a real home." To some degree, of course, all the guest children faced changed circumstances at home. Even if they returned to the same house they had left, to parents still married and with no new brothers or sisters to meet, they and their parents had four or five years of separation to overcome.

Some of the guest children did not want to go home. A man who returned to Britain at age thirteen recalls that he was "devastated. One of the worst, if not the most unhappiest, days of my whole life. Felt I was leaving everything that was dear to me." Judith had been only two when she left home and "did not want to go back." Older children had their own reasons for wanting to stay. Fourteen-year-old Chris "did not want to go home and leave my first girl friend and all the good times I was having." Fourteen-year-old Jean was "very upset as I had become totally involved in Canadian life and did not know what I was going home to." Family obligation influenced some of the guest children, especially the older girls, to return to Britain. A fourteen-year-old girl, who had been unhappy at home, did not want to return. Her foster parents invited her to stay but her mother was in poor health and wanted her home. Home she went, where she was "very unhappy for five years." It was not only children who hesitated to return. One British mother who had settled in Canada was reported in 1946 to have "learned to love the country and the position held by women in Canada and to be unwilling to relinquish it for life in England where the position of women is so different."[12]

Childcare agencies assumed that parents would welcome their children home. There were signs, however, that this would not always be the case. Long breaks in correspondence, forgotten birthdays and arrears in support contributions all suggested that a few parents were glad to let someone else care for their children. In a few, rare cases, the parents seemed willing to abandon their children. One Canadian mother who had cared for three privately evacuated children was disturbed as months went by after the war with no suggestion that the children should come home. When she wrote to the parents, they expressed surprise that she wanted the children to leave. Many months after the war, they agreed that the youngest child could go home. They then wrote to say they could not afford to bring their older children home. More months passed before they agreed to allow the foster mother to take the children to a relative. They were finally put on a ship and sent home at their relative's expense. There were few cases where the bonds of affection were as completely absent as this, but some parents did try to arrange the children's lives to their own advantage. One mother wrote to tell her older daughter to leave school and begin earning money to send home. The younger child was ordered not to come home before she was old enough to work because she would be a burden to the family. Her response was "if they don't want me when I can't earn money, they won't get me when I can." The children remained in Canada and were adopted by their foster parents.

Parents who wanted their children home often declined to consent to their return before the end of the war. Isobel Harvey wanted a boy sent home from British Columbia in 1944 before he "did something delinquent which would give an unfavorable impression in the country of overseas children," but she could do nothing without the parents' consent. The understandable reason most parents had for not allowing children to leave for home was fear for their safety. Memories of the dangers that had halted the evacuation were still vivid in 1944, and parents preferred to wait a few months to be sure that they would see their children again. Some parents said that it would be best for their children to stay in Canada to take advantage of the opportunities it offered, and by 1944, there were many mothers and fathers who hoped to join their children in Canada for a fresh start of their own in the post-war world.

CORB and Canadian agencies helped children to stay in Canada when a return home seemed only to promise trouble. The younger children of one family were allowed to stay with their foster parents after the oldest child returned to England to find a broken home and an alcoholic mother waiting for him. Experiences with the older children who returned home first made CORB more willing to allow some evacuees to stay in Canada if the opportunities for the children were better than what awaited them in Britain. One youth, who was self-supporting, was allowed to settle in Canada because of "experience with boys of [his] age returned to the U.K. against their will [who] have created quite a problem." Staying on proved the best option for some children and their families.[13]

Marjorie Maxse found that most CORB parents were willing to let their sons stay in their host country but that "the girls appear to be expected to return." Ten percent of the parents seriously considered emigrating to join their children. Dominion governments were prepared to welcome the families and F.C. Blair, in his last days at work, assured the British High Commissioner that he would welcome guest children who were not problem cases to stay and be joined by their families. An Order-in-Council allowed guest children who had served in the Canadian forces to immigrate and a number did settle in Canada. The overwhelming majority of guest children, however, went home. By February 1945, all but 205 of the CORB children had gone. Many of them left with plans to return, and many more would make plans after a short time at home.[14]

Departure often followed months of waiting. Even after the war was over, transatlantic ships were crowded and waiting lists long and governed by priorities. The pattern of long waits and sudden departures was a common experience. Many guest children had three days' notice or less that, this time, they really were on their way. The last days were filled with packing and a round of goodbyes. Sometimes a whole community became involved, and in one small town, all the women gathered one day for a sewing party to label the clothes of the two guest children about to leave. Community groups, schools, friends and family clubbed together to see the children off and give them presents. Suddenly, the guest children were news again, and once security restrictions were lifted, the local papers filled with stories of the return.

The foster families watched their guests leave with regret. Some foster parents recall that their regret was mixed with relief at the sudden lifting of responsibility. One foster mother had sworn that she would treat looking after her child as a duty and would not allow herself to become fond of the boy. Over the years, however, she grew very attached to him. In early 1945, the boy learned that he had to return to Britain. He was distraught and longed to stay in Canada; when he found that it was impossible, he became very difficult to handle. His foster mother remained very fond of him but suddenly felt too old to cope, and she was relieved to see him leave for home. A number of foster parents shared the mingled senses of relief and regret and the feeling of exhaustion after five years of caring for a child.

The voyage home on the *Rangitata*, the *Louis Pasteur* or one of the other surviving ships held little of the excitement of the voyage to Canada. The ships were shabby after five years of hard use. The guest children were older, and the contrast between life ashore and life at sea was less marked than it had been in 1940 when they left behind the blackout and the blitz. For those who sailed after May 1945, there was no anxiety about U-boats, no nights spent fully dressed and strapped into lifejackets. Home occupied their thoughts, and the arrival in Glasgow or Liverpool overshadows the details of the voyage in the memories of most evacuees. Canada had greeted them with blazing lights, huge trains and mountains of food. Britain welcomed them home to drab and blitzed cities, tiny trains and rationing beyond anything they had known in Canada.

"Gray, raining Liverpool docks. Everything was very dark and drab with blackout," one guest who returned in wartime recalls. A thirteen-year-old found England "dirty, cold, inhospitable. Hated it all." A twelve-year-old girl noticed the "shoddy, war-weary, tiny houses and neat gardens, very green grass. Everything seemed on a small scale." Tim, coming home from Windsor, Ontario, and life with the President of Ford, found a sharp contrast in Britain: "the lower standard of living, smaller and more old-fashioned cars, no central heating, no fridge." For Patricia, "returning to England was really a nightmare, as it was physically very tough for people who had lived in centrally heated houses (75°) to feel comfortable in English houses, which at the best of times were cold and draughty, but at the end of the war there was nothing to heat the houses with. I remember intense cold *inside*, which was new, and the food was at its very worst in 1944–45."

Nothing could prepare the returning children for the shortages they would face at home. For one child, the first clue came when her parents stared at the sandwiches she brought with her from the boat "made with *white* bread, whiter than they'd seen for a good long time." For most, the first hint came with gifts of chocolate. Dudley, travelling from Gourock to London, was given a bar of chocolate by a soldier on the train and told he "wouldn't see much more in future." Mary Ann was startled the first time her family sliced up a Mars bar to share around. Many children shared eight-year-old Jean's "resentment when my sweet allowance [was] cut." Even the carefully arranged welcome-home parties could be a shock. Peter's parents "had saved a lot of their rations to give us a cheery welcome home but did not raise our spirits. I must have appeared very ungrateful." Jean's family welcomed her home at a meal where they served "some *awful looking* things for dessert . . . it turned out they were dried bananas."

It took some children a while to grasp the reality of shortages and limited choice. Gladys "was used to getting what I wanted . . . when I was taken to a nearby town for some shoes and I saw a pair in the window . . . they wouldn't take them out — so I wouldn't have any." The temptation to compare what they had left and what they had come home to was one that few children could resist. For war-weary parents entering their fifth year of rationing and making do, it was sometimes hard to take. With time, however, most children adjusted to the meager choices postwar Britain offered and even grew used to the sight of adults riding bicycles — a sight that had startled many of them on their first days back in fuel-starved Britain.[15]

Bombed and grubby buildings, poor food, cold houses and shortages made up the physical world to which the children returned, but their chief concerns were emotional. The voyage home and the arrival were colored by anxiety about meeting their parents and about renewing family connections. Jean, returning to Middlesborough after five years, "didn't recognize my father and when he came forward and put his arm around me I reacted violently. I thought he was a stranger about to abduct me." The first shock of reunion was followed by appraisal. The older children, more than the younger, were struck by their parents' age. Some had grown gray, all were worn by five years of strain and shortage. One teenager was stunned to find her parents *"so old"* and a younger child was annoyed because she "thought my mother was so dowdy compared to my Aunt." The parents faced children who had grown rapidly while they were away. Letters, descriptions and photographs did not prepare the parents fully for the size of the children, especially the teenagers, who greeted them at the docks and stations. David's mother had watched the neighborhood children for five years, trying to imagine how he and his sister would look. The returning guest children, however, tended to be bigger than their British contemporaries. One man still recalls the impression two returning evacuees made in his school because "they were huge." They also spoke differently—even those children who had worked to keep their accents sounded Canadian to their parents. A girl who had spent the war at a residential school returned with an accent that her parents thought "thoroughly Canadian."

Although parents might grudgingly accept their sons' long trousers, it was much more difficult for them to accept the changes in their daughters. Fathers, in particular, were astonished to see the children they had sent away in 1940 return as fashionably dressed women wearing make-up. Girls as young as eleven wore Tangee Natural lipstick, and one came home in "high heels, lipstick, red nails and a trouser suit. Father soon removed them all." A fourteen-year-old girl had "a very pale lipstick scrubbed off me as I got off the train." It took some fathers a long time to accept the changes five years had made in their daughters. One woman recalls her father's "horror at my use of make-up, my choice of clothes" — although she was old enough to have served in the RCAF and was about to enter university in Britain.

Many children astonished their parents with their memories of the homes they had left. A girl who had left home at the age of six watched her mother preparing to go out one evening shortly after her return. The mother put on an evening dress the girl had not seen since 1940, and her daughter said, "why don't you wear those long gloves you used to?" The feeling that they had not been forgotten helped parents to welcome their children home. In some homes nothing had changed. Phyllis was seventeen when she came home to her old room, still decorated with nursery curtains.

Nearly all children and parents felt shy at their first meeting, but for a few guest children it was an immediate relief to be home. A thirteen-year-old girl, who had spent the terms at St. Hilda's and holidays as the guest of Canadian families, was delighted "to have parents again: to be able to say 'please may I have?' and not wait to be asked . . . marvelous to be able to take someone for granted, to really 'belong' to someone again, and to be able to make demands like ordinary children do of their parents." Even among some of the children who settled happily at home, however, there was a sense that things were not as they were before. George recalls feeling comfortable with his family when he returned at the age of eighteen, "but I soon realized that my being in another place for three years had created a small gap in our relationship." Mary Ann "didn't feel that I'd lost out by coming home" and the twelve-year-old girl easily resumed life with her parents. But she discovered over time that the years of separation had taken a toll. Although close to her parents, she found, when she visited her foster parents in the years after the war, that she felt even closer to them.

For a few of the guest children, homecoming was a bitter experience. The gap that all the guest children felt, if only for a brief period, never closed in some families. The children were homesick for Canada, their friends and foster families, and chafed at the restrictions Britain imposed on them. The parents felt they were housing strangers and grew weary of the constant references to Canada. The guest children who returned as Canadian teenagers differed from their British contemporaries. Canada had made them more independent, and many parents commented on this quality in their children. Many, too, were troubled and uneasy with the young adults who now faced them. Yolande discovered that "the years with no shared experience made it extremely difficult. My mother remembered the Canada of her childhood and refused to believe some of the manners and customs which we had been taught." Phyllis, at seventeen, behaved arrogantly, and although she was more independent than other girls of her age, she felt separated from them by being "immature in that I hadn't suffered as so many of my age had."

Another young woman found that nothing at home was as she had imagined it: "I had built up an idealized view of what the return would be like, the sort of man my father was, the role I would play as 'mother' to my sibs. Of course it was a very different scene I met." She felt that she "could not please my father or reach his expectations though I think I tried." Her younger sister was sent to boarding school where she would "learn to be British again" before she had a chance to settle at home. "The return was difficult" and the young woman began her studies at University under the weight of a depression that lasted through the first months of her return.

It was not only the parents who were affected when the guest children came home. Once again, the guest children had to feel their way into a family. Brothers and sisters tended to be less accepting of the returning children than their parents. Mary Ann found her nine-year-old brother jealous of the newcomer, and she found it difficult to deal with a younger brother. In Canada, she had been the younger sister of a tolerant, older foster brother. She never became as close to her own brother as she longed to be. Eight-year-old Penelope had a mixed welcome. Her two-year-old brother was "a complete stranger but friendly and loving," while her older brother "made it clear I was an unwelcome intruder." Judith, who had left home at two, found her family "complete strangers [and] got on very badly" with her sisters and brother who "must have found me very difficult, too." Seventeen-year-old Margot and her sister found their "youngest brother minded our return the most." Used to being alone with their mother, he grew "upset when she discussed things with us instead of him as she would have done previously."

Returning guest children reacted to changes in the family in very personal ways. When Jean found a new baby brother at home "I felt really as if I'd been betrayed and pushed out of my rightful place." It took her years to come to love her brothers, but "we are like separate families. The cousins I lived with in [Canada] seem like brothers and sisters." A young girl who felt her relations with her mother "inhibited by a desire to conceal all the unpleasant things that had happened" during her unhappy years in Canada found it easier to relate with her younger sisters. She now thinks that "mothering" them played a big part in her gradual readjustment to life at home. The returning guest children could sometimes build bonds with their youngest brothers and sisters, but often found that a gap remained between themselves and the older children. A number of the guest children were hurt to discover that the experience of evacuation sometimes separated them from brothers and sisters who had also been in Canada. One twelve-year-old boy found the strain of coming home so great that it was easier for him to become close with a younger sister who had spent the war in Britain than with his brothers and sisters who had also been evacuated to Canada. Many guest children shared the experience of a young girl who found that the years of separation between brothers, sisters and parents meant "we were never again the happy little family we had been before the war."[16]

The guest children made the best adjustments they could to home, family, friends and the difficult conditions of life in post-war Britain. Almost without exception, the guest children found that school was one of the worst experiences of their new life. The school embodied the restrictions and narrowness of British life that grated on the independently minded children. They found the emphasis on hierarchy hard to accept, as were school uniforms, the battery of rules and regulations, and the restrictions on jewelry and make-up. Joyce found her school rules petty. "I disliked having to wear the school uniform and resented not being able to wear my gold signet ring to school. I was the first evacuee to return, and the authorities weren't too sure what to do with me." Some of the children resisted the school atmosphere. Fourteen-year-old Michael had already completed Grade 12 when he left for home in 1943. He returned to an English school for one year, but found it "very difficult to conform to the disciplines of an English single-sex school. I was much too independent. They thought me very wild." Chris "was very bolshie and rebellious during my first two terms at public school. After that, I lost my accent and integrated much better. I was also very homesick for my first term but I had an understanding housemaster who helped a lot. I did not like the very cold Spartan conditions of a war-time school." Mike's return to a British public school was helped by a coincidental meeting. A boy he had become friendly with on the return voyage appeared at Mike's new school on the first day of term. They became good friends because both were "Canadian," and they helped each other to adjust to life in a British boarding school.

Once again, the guest children were curiosities to their schoolmates. British children, however, were less welcoming than Canadians had been. The guest children, too, sometimes felt conscious that they had missed an experience endured by the rest of their classmates. An eighteen-year-old who returned in 1943 recalls she had "always a feeling of guilt that I had been enjoying myself while my parents had been getting on with real life — this not because of any remarks made by others." By 1945, however, there were others prepared to make such remarks. Twelve-year-old

Malcolm, sent as a day boy to a boarding school, "had many fights with kids who called me Lord Haw Haw after William Joyce the traitor." Other children sensed hostility in their classmates "because we had missed the war." There was the usual teasing to be expected. A twelve-year-old boy who went to school in his Canadian clothes "was the laughing stock of the school. I was called 'Canuck' and 'colonial' in a denigrating manner."

And, again, their accents set the guest children apart. Their English accents had provoked some teasing in 1940 but had generally been accepted. Canadian accents positively irritated British children, parents and schoolteachers, who waged a savage campaign of extermination. Penelope "dropped my accent when my brother made it clear that it was not 'cute'." Mary Ann was "told before a full class that I would have to lose that 'dreadful accent.' That hurt and a sensitive teacher should have been aware of it." When Dudley returned to his old school, the headmaster "called me into his office and made the strange remark that I spoke with a Canadian accent and must lose it. I thought it a totally unnecessary remark as mixing with English boys my accent started to naturally change." Accent was too intimate a part of the British social structure for head masters to leave it to chance.

Some teachers helped the guest children to adjust to the old ways, but many children noticed a distance between British teachers and pupils that limited independence rather than encouraging it. Relations with teachers were made more difficult because most guest children found themselves behind their age group in school work. Their entry into Canadian schools had

215

often been eased because they found the work easy; their return to British schools was made more difficult by the gap that had opened. Some children, by missing the entrance examinations for grammar schools, lost their chance for a grammar-school placement and saw their educational opportunities sharply reduced. Others were able to get a place in grammar school only by cramming mathematics and French in the summer of 1945. Most returning guest children felt two years behind their classmates. [17]

Many of the returned guest children kept in touch with their foster families, and a number still correspond with their surviving foster parents and their foster brothers and sisters. Women were more likely than men to keep the contacts alive, and when the years of easy transatlantic travel arrived, reunions became more frequent and the contacts increased. There were a number of guest children, just how many is impossible to guess, who could not settle in Britain after their return. Don found that he could not face a career in the Royal Navy with its "very class-conscious approach." After serving for two years, he returned to Canada where he was joined by his parents and sister, herself a guest child. Min found the years "from twelve to twenty-one a mixed up time" in which she longed to return but could not arrange it. Often family circumstances kept the children, especially the girls, at home. They felt obliged to stay and help their aging or ill parents or to contribute to the support of their brothers and sisters. Jean "was very unhappy for some months and I planned to return to Canada. But my brother also could not settle and . . . I stayed home to look after my mother while my brother returned to

Canada." Joyce waited for her sister to finish her education before leaving for Canada twenty years after the end of the war.

Some families recognized that their children could not settle in Britain and had a better chance in Canada. When foster parents offered a home, parents took the hard decision, as Tony's parents did, to let their children go. Malcolm could not settle down in London when he returned at the age of twelve. He got on well with his parents, but always felt like "a Canadian in England . . . I had a free spirit and difficulty with the old English ways." When he turned sixteen, his parents allowed him to return to his foster home — "a correct decision and I respect my English parents' decision to part with me again."[18]

Returning to Canada did not always end the restlessness that living in two worlds had produced. Many former evacuees have friends who were themselves guest children, and thus shared a childhood experience different to that of their Canadian-born friends. Some of the former guest children now in Canada find their thoughts turning back to Britain as they grow older. For others, who did not have the chance to return to Canada, the consequences have lasted all their lives. Thinking over her experiences, one woman wrote "It made me realize how happy I had been whilst there and that from then on, after returning to England, there has always been a thread of unsettlement running through my life, as though nowhere is really home. Even now, though I have been in this area for nearly twenty-five years and made many friends, I still have a sense of just passing through."

CHAPTER VIII

❖

THE
RETURN VOYAGE

❖

JOHN HUTTON: Age 12
CORB Evacuee

As John prepared to go home in July 1945, Mrs. Pellett tried to sum up her feelings and those of her family now that John was leaving: "It is with mixed emotions to all of us that we receive this news. We have been waiting for so many weeks it seems. We are all so glad that he is returning to his home and yet there is going to be quite an empty space in our home and in our hearts.

"I have been sitting here taking stock, realizing how very long I have had John under my influence and wondering if I have done well with him. I have tried so hard but there have been a number of times when we have not understood each other and have had our disagreements. I hope John will forget these instances and remember only the pleasant ones, the grand talks we've had together (oh, you are going to enjoy talking with him) and the books he, Bobbie and I have read together and the other good things and outings. I am really proud of the boy I am sending back to you. I can answer myself truthfully as to that. He is fine and clean in character and strong and healthy in body. I realize that it must be very difficult for a child to have no mother but I know John is very greatly blessed in having the father he has. He will be a great pal to you, I know. He is the kind of a child one can make a pal of, especially as he is the only one. I'm hoping to arrange a going-away party next week if I can get enough food to eat. Things are getting pretty tight here now. The school has presented John with a fountain pen as a going-away present."

The time of parties and goodbyes passed quickly, and one evening the family drove John to Union Station in Toronto where a party of returning evacuees gathered for the journey home. Emotions were high as many of the children were unhappy at the thought of leaving. John felt sad, but he also looked forward to life in England and to meeting his father once again.

The CORB party travelled to Quebec and boarded the *Stratheden* for the voyage to Liverpool. John was at sea when news came of the atom bomb attacks on Japan: "I cannot recall any great sense of foreboding, indeed there was some jubilation that these bombs would bring the war with Japan to an end." They reached Liverpool on August 11, and had their first contact with postwar Britain. Customs men descended on the party and examined their luggage closely. Many of the children had brought back gifts of clothes for their parents and relatives, which provoked suspicion among the officials. With that welcome behind him, John climbed into the little train waiting at dockside and travelled from Liverpool on a "misty summer morning, through soft green country full of patchwork fields and little houses" heading for Euston station in London.

CORB had telephoned Mr. Hutton only the day before to tell him to meet his son at Euston. He invited John's uncle and his cousin, David, to join him in London. David was about John's age, and Mr. Hutton hoped he would help his son feel "more at his ease than if he were confronted by two grownups." Stepping off the train, John saw his father at once, and it was an emotional moment for them both. His father wrote: "By good fortune we were within a few yards of the door through which John emerged. We recognized each other immediately. I shall never forget his first, 'Oh, Dad.' I knew in that moment that John had always remembered. There was no trace of uncontrolled excitement; just a quiet sense of infinite relief and the tone of those two words answered all the doubts lingering in my mind. During all those long years of separation, John had kept me in his thoughts." The small party rounded up John's luggage and found a taxi to take them across town to Liverpool Street station. They waited for the Colchester train in a tearoom looking down over the crowded platforms. "For the first time, I drank a cup of tea; in Canada children [were] confined to milk." Then it was time for the evening train to Colchester, where another uncle was waiting to collect them in his car. They made a quick visit to a favorite aunt before John was driven to his

221

father's new house, where the elderly housekeeper made a big fuss of him. At supper, John found the food strange; the meal "included plaice, a fish quite unknown to my Canadian palate, served with tartar sauce." As he went up to bed that night, John felt that "after five years' absence, I had returned home."

The next couple of days were hectic. Cousin David spent all his spare time with John, examining the baseball bat, the pennant of the Statue of Liberty and other souvenirs brought back from Canada. Friends and relatives had to be visited, and John impressed many of them with his polite answers to their questions and his "soft Canadian voice." One acquaintance pleased Mr. Hutton by saying that "John is two years in advance of the average English boy in his outlook on life and his general bearing." His father did worry that "with all the interest displayed . . . John will be lucky to escape with a slightly swollen head and his father runs an even greater risk." Then there was all the bureaucratic work to be taken care of— identification cards and ration books—before they were free to take a short welcome-home holiday in London. They left for London on the day after VJ day.

John ran his father ragged in London: "We . . . visited Westminster Abbey, Whitehall, Trafalgar Square and Westminster Bridge, which we watched as it boomed out the hour. His Majesty was in residence at the Palace but did not appear as we had hoped, though the crowd continually let off concerted yells of 'We want the King'.

"John could have stayed all day in the Abbey, reading the inscriptions on the monuments. . . . He was particularly intrigued by the memorial to Wolfe and went back to it once or twice to read the references to Canada cut in the stonework. . . . During our two days in London, I think we tried every kind of transport: trains, with disappointingly small engines; buses, double deckers well-favored as they are not, I gather, seen much in Canada, underground railways, escalators, moving stairways and lifts. In the matter of transport, John expressed surprise that nearly everyone, young and old, has a cycle. He had an impression that cycles are only for the young. He now has one which he thinks is 'smart', a sports model with upturned handle bars. For the first few days he only got off it to eat his meals, but has now settled down to a more normal routine."

As the first excitement of coming home wore off, John began to notice the differences of his new life. The shortages, the drab surroundings and the strange food were bearable, and he reveled in the bike rides through the "manicured countryside," but he had returned from Canada "very independently minded and with a broader view of life" than he found among his contemporaries. The rigidities and assumptions of English life began to grate. The full weight of English tradition hit him when he began school in September. The school was Colchester Royal Grammar School and it proved a very different world from Agincourt. His father wrote: "It is one of the three senior schools in the town. Normally admittance is by examination only, but I pleaded special circumstances and after an interview with the headmaster, John was accepted. The Grammar schools are usually regarded as offering the best facilities for boys whose abilities are above the average. Homework [is] an innovation which John

223

regards as an imposition, though I have no doubt he will accept it as part of the game. . . . The other is the prefect system, definitely a bone of contention. Selected senior boys of the school are appointed as prefects. The selection is partly by the seniors themselves and partly by the staff. To these prefects is delegated the responsibility of overseeing the conduct of the lads at the school. There is some difference of opinion about the matter, some thinking the system beneficial as it gives the boys an interest in the welfare of the school while others contend that it gives the prefects an exalted opinion of their own importance and is an incentive to petty tyranny. Be that as it may, John is definitely opposed to the system and I do not think he will change his opinion—until he becomes a prefect. John has been placed in the lowest class for one week but this is to be reviewed next Monday when John will be given an opportunity to express an opinion to the Head. If John thinks he should be in a higher class and the form master agrees, the matter will be arranged."

John continued to eat heartily, which was a problem in 1945. As his father wrote, "The immediate problems are clothing and feeding. I have managed to get him fitted out in the usual style for boys of his size, if not his age; gray flannel trousers and a loose-fitting sports jacket. The suit he came home in we are keeping for special occasions. His appetite is a source of perpetual wonder. He can eat and he does enjoy his food."

School brought new friends, and his widower father's "sedate household" was soon invaded by young boys stopping in for tea. John began to play rugby and to adjust to the routine of school life. As soon as his father had scraped up the coupons for a school tie, John added it to his outfit and "flaunts the tie and swears the Grammar school is the best in town." Even the prefects seemed more tolerable on closer acquaintance. But just as there had been a tension under the apparently calm adjustment to life in Agincourt, so there was strain in his return to Colchester. He was irritated and unengaged by school: "I lost motivation for some years." It was a full three years after his return that John felt at home in Britain.

NINA LAVILLE: Age 16
CORB Evacuee

"I think if there had been brothers or sisters I would *never* have returned to England. I felt it was my duty to return being an only child." Nina was among the last of the CORB children to leave Canada. "When peace was declared I knew it would soon be time to go back to England." Word came in August 1945 that the journey had been arranged and Nina "was devastated," and very anxious about the reunion with her parents. "When I left England, I was a timid eleven-year-old child . . . when I returned, I was a rather attractive sixteen-year-old. I could converse with anyone and hold my own in any conversation. I liked the boys and they liked me."

Nina's parents thought she "was too forward" and the reunion was as difficult as she had feared. For five years, her parents had lived alone together and "had been used to being without me. I felt as though I was an intrusion. My father was jealous of my relationship

with my mother. I must say that I didn't really want
to be there — I wanted to be back in Canada. I did tend
to compare my life in England with the life in Canada,
and England seemed claustrophobic and dirty. I
couldn't believe the dirt and grime on buildings. I had
no friends, and when I did get in touch with old school
chums, I think I was a bit brash and full of how good
things were in Canada — quite the wrong approach."
Nina could not face going back to school, and instead
trained as a comptometer operator. She worked in an
office, living uncomfortably at home until she married
in 1952. The ties to Canada remained strong. She
wrote regularly to her friends and relatives there, met
them when they visited Britain on holidays over the
next forty years, but never returned to her foster
country. "The five years I was in Canada were very
happy years, and after I returned, things were never
the same again."

DAVID BROWN: Age 12
Rotary Evacuee

"We received your telegram last Wednesday and
I am very excited. The Rotary Club thinks it will be
only a matter of weeks before we leave. Janette is also
very excited and will be glad to see you again. On
Saturday, Mrs. Luke bought me two pairs of long pants
which I keep as my best although when I come home
I will be wearing them. My thoughts now are mostly
of going home but I am keeping it secret until definite
arrangements are made," David wrote home,
decorating his letter with a picture of a ship racing
toward Britain.

The Browns were as excited as their children at the prospect of reunion. Mr. Brown wrote to the Rotary Committee chairman to explain his mood and express his thanks. "My wife and I are getting very excited at the prospect of having David and Janette with us again, and are making all the arrangements for their welfare in this country. One of the most difficult is the housing problem, but we will have overcome this before they arrive.

"I don't know how to start to thank you all for your marvelous kindnesses to them, and us, but that will be the subject of further correspondence in the future. From the time we received Morley Luke's original cable announcing David and Janette's safe arrival, we felt we had made the correct decision in accepting your invitation, and we had complete confidence that their welfare under the guidance of your Rotary Club would be well looked after.

"My wife and I proceeded to spend all our time and energies on war work and what with Home Guard and fire-watching duties carried out in our 'spare' time we quite often did not see one another for several days, although living in the same house. You are probably aware that my work is in the aircraft industry and my wife immediately took up work in a radio (in its broadest sense) factory, and has built up a whole shop of about fifty girls manufacturing radio valves, of which she has been the working head. Had not you taken care of our children she would not have been able to do this job of work for the war.

"What a wonderful influence on the future well-being and understanding within the British Commonwealth will have been made by these British citizens having lived in Canada and other parts of the Empire during their youth. The problems in the future appear to be very complex, but if only the British Nations can pull together, I am sure their influence on the world for good will be far-reaching. Of course, Rotary has a wonderful chance of doing good work along these lines and we are very conscious of this in our Club.

"In my letter to Morley Luke, I suggested that David and Janette return in late spring or early summer, but now we hope they will be able to return much earlier.

"We still get, as you will have read in the papers, quite a bit of enemy action, but so far we have had no damage done to the house in which we live with my father-in-law, and hope by the time David and Janette return it will have passed."

Arrangements were quickly made, and within a month the return David "had been anticipating with longing for at least two years" began. David and his sister took the train to New York on February 1, 1945, in the charge of a Red Cross nurse. Once there, they went immediately to the *Rangitata*. They spent three days in New York Harbor, and a quick camaraderie sprang up between the boys in David's dormitory: "We organized a Society that we called the Independent Society of Fishballs as there were already Hamburgers, Meatballs, etc." At noon of the fourth day on board, the ship set sail.

David found the twelve-day voyage to Liverpool tedious. In his diary of "My trip to England," he listed deck games in the morning, card games in the afternoon, bingo and games in the evening. The high

228

point of some days was having a bath. David wanted the trip to end and to be home once again. After ten long days at sea, "we went on deck one afternoon and saw land. Everyone started singing 'Don't fence me in.' Now the very thought of the song reminds me of that happiest time of my life." The next day, they entered the Liverpool Channel, and passed submarines and warships waiting at the mouth of the Mersey. Their journey was not yet over, since the *Rangitata* was forced to anchor in the river for three days while waiting for a berth. Finally, on February 19, "We got up early and left the boat at seven-thirty. At ten-thirty, our train started on a boring trip till three-thirty, when for the first time in four years we met our parents."

"My immediate impressions were that my family were not quite as I had remembered them." Their parents commented on their Canadian accents and on the fact that they were "older and bigger," but made no great fuss about their Canadian ways. After nearly five years away, it took David "two or three months to fall into the new ways. It was now that the differences in family dynamics were most noticeable. In many ways, my foster parents had done an excellent job in keeping me aware of the differences that I might expect on my return. As they had never met my family, they were not always right but they made worthwhile attempts." David found that his emotional adjustment to a "new" family was rapid, and the Browns welcomed their children warmly.

But the demands of the public school to which he was sent left much to be desired. There "my accent and lack of English vocabulary (for example, the technical terms of cricket) continued to trouble me for about three years. Some words have different meanings and some things were called by different names. The long English 'a' caused me to pause before pronouncing a word to make sure I got it right. In school work I was well behind in Math and Latin. Math I picked up in six months. Latin was a lost cause." David did not suffer academically; school led to university and ultimately to a doctoral degree.

After his return, David continued to write to his foster parents and often "recalled the long warm Canadian summers," although he had no urge to return. He planned a holiday visit in 1953, but nothing came of it. "When I did return, the decision was intellectual not emotional—only to a small extent affected by my Montreal childhood and then it was more out of curiosity to see whether Canada was as I remembered it." David returned to Canada in 1959, when he was offered a three-year postdoctoral fellowship. "My parents feared that I might marry and settle in Canada." They were correct. David still lives in Ontario.

MARY ANN WAGHORN: Age 12
CORB Evacuee

"This was the time for which I had waited so long. I certainly don't recall that I ever waited with any degree of impatience and I cannot help wondering if my joyous reaction was rather conditioned. I had been nothing but happy with my foster family and had they been less correct in keeping my own family so much in mind, I cannot help thinking I would happily have stayed with them." Mary Ann's foster parents took her to Toronto's Union Station almost five years to the day after she reached Canada. They said goodbye to her in the concourse and parted with her at the gate to the platform. The newspapers were there, and a photographer told a group of parents to wave and smile goodbye. As she watched her foster daughter disappear into the crowd of children, Mrs. Mann waved goodbye with one hand while she balled a handkerchief in the other.

Mary Ann spent a week on the *Louis Pasteur* thinking about the reunion ahead. "I guess I didn't really know what to expect." Her parents were waiting for her as she got off the train and greeted her warmly. Happy that her daughter appeared so little changed, her mother "wrote to my Aunt and thanked her specially for keeping me so much the same. I had gone out in 1940 with long hair in braids and came home still with long hair. . . . Only the accent and my height were different."

The large family of aunts and uncles "rallied round and eased me back into the swing of things again" and her reunion with her parents went "easily and comfortably." The reunion with her brother was not so easy. Only three years old when Mary Ann left home, he now barely remembered her—even though they had written to each other. "He had my parents to himself and understandably resented an older newcomer. I found it difficult to adjust to a younger brother after a tolerant and caring older one. Jealousy reared its head and we argued a good deal and fought also, to my shame. However, in time we settled down together. To be honest, even now I am not as close to my brother as I feel I should be, and I am inclined to put this down to the fact that we were separated for five of our early years. Whereas although I've only seen my Canadian 'brother' three times since the war, I feel a comfortable affinity with him. And although I was close to my parents I felt far closer and more at ease with my foster parents on the four occasions we met after the war." Mary Ann wrote monthly letters to her foster parents and remained in close touch for the next forty years.

Outside home, Mary Ann "was intrigued by prisoners of war working in the streets, windows criss-crossed with protective tape, that sort of thing." "Settling to school was probably the greatest hurdle to overcome;" but she won a place at the local grammar school, bought her new uniform and was given a new bike to ride. "I'm afraid the reality of the whole thing was a bitter disappointment. I joined my classmates in their second year at school and I was somewhat in their wake. Whereas I was easily accepted into my Canadian school and happily adjusted to school life, this was not the case in reverse. I was most unhappy. There was vague mention of changing schools but how could I disappoint my folks? I stuck [with] it."

THE CURTIS FAMILY
CORB Evacuees

Hazel was seventeen when she went home, Muriel sixteen, Fred fourteen and the twins eleven. Hazel had left Winnipeg in 1944 "sad to leave my brothers and sister but glad to be going home." Her parents welcomed her home and remarked on her accent and "the fact that I was a grown-up daughter and not the young teenager who went away." The war was still on when she reached Britain and it "seemed pretty grim. V1 [bombs] were just beginning and the V2 [bombs] were yet to come. The blackout seemed awful and the rationing of food—but everyone was in good spirits." Arriving in the midst of war meant that Hazel was soon plunged into the same kind of war work that her parents were doing, and that helped her to adjust to life at home. During the day she worked at her new job in a bank, and after work she "enjoyed the comradeship with all types of people doing whatever jobs we had to do—firewatching, helping the elderly or whatever." By the time her sister and brothers returned, Hazel felt fully at home.

Muriel looked forward to meeting her mother and father and two brothers again, but Fred had "mixed feelings" about going home. The twins thought going home was "terrific," but shortly after they reached Chelmsford, they began to have doubts. Muriel found Britain "very small and dark, as blackout was still enforced." It was "difficult being in a small house with such a large family," but generally she found it easy to adjust. Fred, too, found it a big jump from the large quiet house with his retired foster parents to "being surrounded by a large family" and living with nine people in a small house. At fourteen, he was restless, and delighted in the discovery that he was also old enough "to leave school and start work, which I did." As soon as he was old enough, he joined the Marines.

Tony and Geoffrey had the greatest difficulty rejoining the family in Chelmsford. Tony had not recognized his parents when they met the train at

Chelmsford station, and he never overcame the feeling that "they were not our parents." Mrs. Curtis had gone out to work during the war, partly to raise the money for the weekly payments to CORB. There were no servants or cars at home now, and Geoffrey found his family's financial and social standing hard to accept. The house was jammed with people, half of whom were strangers to the twins, and they began to show their resentment as they came under the discipline of their "stern but loving father."

Hazel welcomed them home, and they respected and loved her. They called her "the Manager" and looked to her for help and advice as they struggled with their problems. She was the one who interceded with their parents and tried to keep the peace between the children. Tony felt distant from his brothers who had stayed at home and believed that they were jealous of those who had gone to Canada. He found it hard to think of the seven of them as "brothers and sisters at all as we were all brought up by four different families." The twins' sense of separateness was reinforced by their continuing contacts with the Rosses. During the grim first days of peace, rationing grew more severe than it had been during even the worst days of war, and a steady stream of food parcels arrived from Winnipeg. They were "always addressed to Tony and Geoffrey, not to the family." The other children got no parcels from their Canadian families. The food was shared, but the parcels did seem to widen the gap between the twins and their brothers and sisters.

Above all, they were kept apart by their feeling that they were only visiting. In 1946, the Rosses wrote to the Curtises to suggest that the twins return to

Winnipeg to finish school and possibly to settle in Canada. "Mother and Father unselfishly let them return," Hazel noted. It was not easy to arrange the return to Canada of two young children, and it required negotiations between the Rosses and some British friends in Winnipeg to cut the red tape. Meanwhile the boys went to school in Chelmsford.

Finally, in May 1948, Tony and Geoff said their goodbyes and took the train to Liverpool. They reached Winnipeg in time for the May 24th holiday. Their pictures appeared in the paper again, and all their old teachers phoned the Ross home to welcome them back. "It was amazing." The Ross family was as warm as ever, and the twins settled in happily to take up their lives again with the family. They graduated, remained in Canada, and made their lives in the country. Tony went often to Britain on business and always visited his family. As the years went by, he began to feel closer to the Curtises and the gap between them, so wide in 1945, gradually closed.

JOHN JARVIS: Age 9
CORB Evacuee

"Early in 1945 I was told I would be going back to England to see my parents. To this day I cannot think how I felt then. It just didn't register. I knew it was going to be an adventure. My brother Michael was with me and though I hadn't seen a lot of him, I know I trusted him implicitly." For John, going home was more of a wrench than leaving Southport had been. He had grown to love Mrs. Jarvis "and really did not know my own mother." Nor did he fully grasp that he might be saying goodbye to Grimsby forever. "I don't think I realized that I wasn't going to be back after the 'holiday'." When the boys went to the station one April evening, it "seemed like the whole town was there" to say goodbye.

The CORB party gathered in Montreal for the trip to New York, where, along with other returning evacuees from the United States and Canada, they boarded the *Rangitata*. "Some of them were not very happy to be going back and others seemed to be glad they were going. It may have been the first time I realized that some people hadn't had as happy a life as I did in North America." The voyage home was marked by news of the death of President Roosevelt, which meant little to John but left "the older people (which was just about everybody else) in a sort of awed grief." A reminder that the war was not yet over came when they practiced life-boat drills and "stood on deck with life jackets on as we neared the British Isles." One day near the end of the voyage, John saw "two oil tankers on fire near the horizon." He was glad to reach the Mersey and watch the unfamiliar landscape slipping by as the *Rangitata* headed for Liverpool.

"Michael knew everything worth knowing and pointed out the English houses and churches which looked to be either green or gray. I then got very nervous about meeting my parents, mostly because there seemed to be an awful lot of people on the wharf and we leant over the rails with our pictures of them and thought we would be in a tight spot if we didn't recognize them. When we walked through the crowds we were both pretty scared but Michael said 'There's

Dad' and I recognized Mother at the same time so it all went off pretty well." They were soon home again and getting to know one another. "It took us both some time to adjust. Everyone spoke so fast (they of course thought we would go to sleep before we finished a sentence)."

"School was the most difficult . . . writing with a dip ink pen. I used to be near the top of my class in Canada, but found I was out of my depth, so they gave me special studies where I had to swot up . . . eventually, I must have caught up as I passed a scholarship to the Grammar School when I was eleven." Michael became "an apprentice engineer and went to sea as soon as my father couldn't stop him."

John stayed in touch with both of his Canadian families. Mrs. Foster "returned to England to live with her sister some years after the war ended and we all used to go over and visit her and her sister about once every three months. She had a soft spot for me and I for her." The Jarvises wrote regularly, and Mr. Jarvis visited England a number of times after the war, as did John's foster sisters. John himself went to sea when he was sixteen, but nearly forty years passed before he returned to Canada for a holiday among his old friends. The Jarvis home "had been pulled down," but Mrs. Foster's homes still stood and "the farms and hill we used to toboggan down, which didn't seem so steep as I remember," were recognizable. To John, everything reminded him of a time that had come to seem "all golden sunshine now."

BETTY HEELEY: Age 14
Rotary Evacuee

By 1944, Betty felt completely at home in Windsor. She had begun her second year at Walkerville Secondary School and spoke and dressed like any other teenager. She had felt like a Canadian for a long time, and her teachers treated her as a regular student. She felt close to her foster family and her many friends in Windsor, and while she never felt that she had lost touch with her mother and father in Yorkshire, they were thousands of miles away and linked by an erratic correspondence. One day that correspondence brought grave news. Her grandmother was in hospital for an operation. A second operation followed and, at the end of 1944, it was clear to the Heeleys that Nana was dying. They asked Rotary to arrange for the children to go home as quickly as possible and in January 1945, Michael left for home.

It was a difficult time. Betty did not know how gravely ill her grandmother was, and she felt "very torn" at the thought of leaving her foster home. Despite the love and attention she had in that home, however, she felt "I was by myself in Canada" once Michael left. "One morning, I realized I couldn't phone him and I had a three-year-old brother I'd never seen." She was ready to go home. Two weeks after Michael had left, Betty said goodbye and took the train back to Montreal. Those two weeks had passed in an exhausting round of goodbye visits. "My dear Aunt Edith and Uncle Ross never let me see a sad expression or a flicker of pain. I was taken to see all the people and places I wished, and after I was put on the train, Edith collapsed and was bedfast for three weeks." Betty joined the Rotary children gathered at the station and boarded a special sleeper train where cars A-R had been reserved for the trip to New York. Once in New York, Betty was assigned a berth, and when she reached her bunk on the ship, she found Brenda and Paddy in the same section. The friends were reunited for the voyage home.

It was a miserable voyage with "bad food and bad facilities," and when the ship reached Liverpool the port was so crowded that they had to anchor in the Mersey for three days. It was Monday morning before the children were brought ashore and Betty was put on the train to Huddersfield. Her father met her at the station with the news that Nana had died on Sunday night, and Betty's thrill at being home dissolved into shock. Her first day at home was the day of her grandmother's funeral, and she spent it stunned and irritated by the constant stream of friends and relatives who all seemed to open their conversation with "I bet you don't remember me."

When the parents and children were at last alone together their own reunion went well. Timothy was a help: "having a younger unknown brother probably gave us all something else to focus on" and eased the tensions of the early days. Timothy had some trouble grasping that Betty was his sister. "He always called me Bettyheeley and said Bettyheeley says" whenever she pronounced a word he did not understand in her strange Canadian accent. Mr. Heeley was "terribly glad" to see his children again and they adjusted easily to life at home.

But England seemed small and drab. "Everything seemed smaller" and the blackout was still in effect.

Rationing was much more severe than it had been in 1940 or was still in Canada, and the run-down air of Britain made a sharp contrast with Windsor. The sharpest contrast of all was at school. Mr. Heeley spoke to the local grammar school headmaster for advice about how Michael and Betty could get up to standard for entry. He was told: "You should never have sent them to Canada." Michael had private tuition in French, arithmetic and Latin and then went away to school, while Betty was admitted to the grammar school; "It was traumatic." She was behind in some subjects but ahead in others and "I always felt awkward, some of the children picked on me." The regulations and school rules were never explained to her before she broke them. She learned that she had to wear the school hat, and she was reported for talking to boys at the bus stop. "They were neighbors and my brother's friends, and I couldn't see the sense in cutting them dead at the bus stop."

Things were not the same at home in 1945. Betty's brother begged his father to emigrate, but Mr. Heeley knew he could not practise in Canada and he knew, too, that his health was frail. The Hardys "wrote and sent lovely parcels until after rationing ceased" and Betty felt torn between home and Windsor. She also sensed her mother's hurt at her affection for Edith. A year after she returned to Britain, Betty's father died and she had a strong feeling that her family was disintegrating — life "was not as it had been in Canada or as she remembered it" in Yorkshire. She grew restless and finally, in 1951, decided to return to Canada. Betty returned to a warm welcome from her foster family and lived with them for a time. But life in Canada proved lonelier than she had expected as "most of my school friends had gone away to University." She found a job and later met and married a man from Scotland. Mr. Hardy gave her away.

FRED: Age 15
CORB Evacuee

During his years in Canada, Fred had "felt 'foreign' when it suited me but generally speaking I felt more Canadian and quite quickly—I didn't want to be different. I tried to speak the same. I believe a lot of the accent came naturally and without any conscious effort." He had written to his parents and never felt that he was losing touch with them during his years in Manitoba. Now he sailed for home with "very mixed feelings—I felt I was being removed from an environment I enjoyed and being forced into something I wasn't sure about—but I chose that rather than go back to the farm."

As a boy seaman in the Royal Navy, Fred was sent to New York to make the journey home on the old *Queen Elizabeth*. She "arrived in the Clyde on a very bleak day—everything looked so dismal" and Fred's homecoming was "in a word—shattering. Because of the severe food rationing the food was not comparable with what I'd been used to in Canada. Everything looked small in comparison—the houses, trains, cars." He spent his short leave in Middlesborough before reporting to his ship.

Despite the first shattering impressions of the Clyde, Fred found that it was quite easy to readjust to life in Britain. "I'd had to adjust and readjust so many times in my life that I just took everything as it came." His parents commented on "my size, my accent and the fact that I'd grown up very quickly." The reunion was an easy one and they all got on "very well," but Fred was not home for long. He soon had to report to the depot and for the next two years "I didn't see too much of them — leaves weren't too frequent" during the war. He served in the Royal Navy for ten years after the war before returning to Middlesborough. He did not keep in touch with his uncle.

GRANIA O'BRIEN: Age 15
Lady Eden's School

The news that she was to leave Canada for home made Grania "very apprehensive, because it would be starting a new life: parents who were strangers and a new school, new home, new friends to make." The years at Chaudière House had brought the children and adults close together, and Grania was reluctant to say goodbye to Lady Eden. To add to her worries about what awaited her at home was the fact that she would be in charge of four younger children on the journey home "unaccompanied by an adult." At the time, returning ships had no space for children too young to join the forces. Instead, they would sail from New York on a Portuguese ship to Lisbon and fly from there to England. Lady Eden and some of the Breakeys drove the children to Quebec to catch the train, and they said their goodbyes at the station.

Despite Grania's fears, the voyage home was uneventful and the delay in Lisbon short. Soon Grania was flying to Bristol; from there, she caught the train for London. Equipped with only an address, she made her way alone to the strange new home. When her father arrived some time later, "he didn't know who I was . . . my mother said that she wouldn't have known me. They didn't quite know how to treat me as I had grown from a child of twelve to nearly adult fifteen. I had grown shy and serious." It was an awkward reunion made more difficult by the move to Ireland and the unfamiliar surroundings. It took "a few months of getting to know each other again until we got on as well and as happily as before I left them three years previously."

There was one place in which Grania never felt happy after her return. At the end of the summer holidays, she was sent to boarding school in England and "was very unhappy. I had been used to responsibility and had lived as one large family in Canada, so I resented the restrictions. Also having done more cooking than lessons for a year, I was a year older than my classmates, which at that time I felt deeply. There were a few other ex-evacuees at the school, and we were faintly despised for having been sent away from England." It was hard to readjust to English life and Grania found the country "drab, the people intense and unsmiling, the food was terrible — I couldn't understand the excitement when each child was issued with half a banana for the first time." Life in Ireland, with no blackout and more abundant food, was a happy escape, and in the holidays, Grania gratefully returned to her new home. In later years she made her own home in Ireland and, despite a desire to see the country, never again visited Canada.

HAZEL WILSON: Age 18
CORB Evacuee

"Mother's first words were 'Thank goodness you don't have a Yankee accent'." Hazel and her brother returned to Colchester as a young woman and young man: "I went home with plenty of nylons and high heels — a big asset in England in 1944. Father wanted to know about the whole four years. He acted as if he wished he could have gone. I think Mother thought a modern daughter was too much sometimes." The Wilsons had always been a close family, and both the children felt grateful to their parents and eager to re-establish the old links and forge new ones with the sister who barely remembered them. "It's swell to be home" Hazel wrote in her diary.

Her mood did not last. Britain was drab: "The sky was too low, no bright sunshine." Her brother left to serve in the Royal Navy. Trips to the Labour Exchange showed "I was much too good for any jobs I could get. I had to go to London to get something worthwhile. There were none in Colchester at all." Hazel had had friends and dates in Winnipeg, but now days went by with barely any social contact. "Still nothing to do — I am getting sick of this" she wrote in her diary in February 1945, and, a month later, "What a dull life. Nothing at all to write about except work." She was in London for VE day in May, sitting on the curb in Trafalgar Square at two o'clock in the morning waiting for the Victory Parade to pass by about noon, and staying on until nightfall to watch the fireworks display in the air over the river Thames. She could share the elation of that day, but she could not shake off the restless dissatisfaction that engulfed her. Back home, she felt Canadian and out of place, her speech and writing dotted with carefully preserved Canadianisms. The only solution lay in Canada, and in March 1946, she went to Canada House to inquire about emigrating. Early in 1947, she returned to the Rooks' home in Winnipeg and to her old job at the Liquor Commission. "I thought she would come back," Mrs. Rook told the local paper. "I could tell by her letters she missed Canada and all she learned to like while she was here." By 1955 all of her family had settled in Canada.

CYNTHIA LORD: Age 16
St. Hilda's School

"When we got home on Monday I found a lovely long letter waiting from Mummie—May 1st. Thank you ever so much. You said I was coming home soon. You know Dr. Dobson gave Uncle Dick and Uncle Ed the impression we *would* have to wait until we were seventeen like everyone else. I was quite prepared to do so. In the meantime I would be able to graduate from Alma with a diploma in Junior Matric. You know that *would* mean an awful lot to anyone. But the best years of my childhood so to speak should not be given to 'adoptive parents' should they? I understand how you feel. And yet I, too, feel the same way. I cannot make up my mind though what would be best—to come home now—to danger and my own parents—or stay here and graduate. You know I have simply too many friends out here—and sometimes it seems the love of them and of Alma is trying to pull me away from the normal life I want so much at home. I could live two lives. The thing I hate about *one*, is going to an English school with snobs and prefects . . . I guess I'm scared. But then to stay away from home for another year would be awful. I can't go to an English boarding school. Come to Canada, Alma, Cobourg and you *would* understand."

By June 1944, Cynthia was resigned to going home and wrote to her parents about "the biggest thing that ever happened." Dr. Dobson, the principal, had told some of the English girls that they "had to be sufficient[ly] prepared so that any time in June we could be ready to leave within 24 hours' notice. He told us both afterwards not to be too excited, but in case it really did happen to be ready. He thinks we will go, and that he is going to miss us an awful lot. Gee, I only hope it's true . . . We are so excited—everyone knows and they all said they were going to miss us . . . I just cried like anything. I was so happy . . . I think I would die if I couldn't go home after all this . . . Oh, just think—maybe I will even get home before this letter. Maybe I won't but it's a wonderful hope I've got anyway." The hope came to nothing, however, and Cynthia did not leave for home until 1945. By then, she "hated to go home, I loved my sponsors and had a very nice boyfriend . . . and I would have been quite happy to stay and finish my education."

On her sixteenth birthday, Cynthia sailed for home, unsure what she would find, reluctant to leave her friends but eager to be reunited with her parents and with her brother, who had recently graduated from medical school.

When Cynthia came down the gangplank wearing her Canadian clothes, her nylon stockings and her make-up, she found her parents unprepared for the changes in their daughter. Nor was she completely ready for the changes wrought by the war. Cynthia noticed at once that her parents "were gray-haired, at least father was, mother still had some hair dye about." After the first hesitations, however, everything went smoothly. "I think I just dropped back into the general routine. My brother was very pleased to take me about to dances and to introduce me to his friends, which was lovely for me. I loved being home with my parents and adored my brother. There were blackouts, and no petrol, but when the sky lit up at night from the steelworks I knew I was at home."

Cynthia's parents made it plain that they were delighted to have her home. She talked to her mother about fashions and "Mother always said that the Canadian girls were very pretty, perhaps this was due to the fact that they had all the make-up and nylons and clothes that the English girls had been deprived of." Mr. Lord accepted his Canadian teenaged daughter, although he criticized some of her habits — especially her table manners — and he "sometimes corrected my pronunciation. They always felt that they had lost a great deal by sending me away."

With a warm and welcoming home, Cynthia found it quite easy to adjust to life in Britain in her first weeks. The hardest adjustment came when she returned to school: "I refused to go to a boarding school, and went to a local grammar school. At sixteen, imagine, no make-up, black stockings and tunics. Boys, awful immature school boys. I absolutely hated school and I was so far behind in maths. We had never done any geography other than Canada and the same with history; we had done no European history at all, my French was all spoken with a wrong accent. I was good at domestic subjects, but even the Art that I loved was no good here. I did get the equivalent of nine O levels after a year, but that was only because I hated it all so much I was determined to get the hell out of school as soon as I could. Some of my former friends were unkind about me deserting my country, but I soon decided they were only jealous."

In later years, Cynthia realized that she had never completely accepted life in England. She stayed in touch with her Cobourg family, and she and Helen, still friends despite their childhood spats, managed separate visits to them from time to time over the next forty years. Each visit renewed Cynthia's dreams of emigrating to Canada, and she took her husband with her on one trip to look into the possibilities. Nothing came of it, and Cynthia went back to Britain knowing that "I would go at the drop of a hat if I had the chance even now."

Where Are They Now?

Today, the guest children are scattered around the world. John Hutton lives in Oxfordshire, England; Nina Laville (Cossins) in the North East of England; David Brown in Ontario, Canada; and Mary Ann Waghorn (Hodgson) in Berkshire, England. Hazel Curtis died in 1985; the twins, Tony and Geoffrey, now live in Ontario; Frederick and Muriel in Essex, England. John Jarvis lives in New Zealand; Betty Heeley (Milne) in Ontario; Fred in the North East of England; Grania O'Brien (Weir) in Ireland; Hazel Wilson (Sands) in the West Indies; and Cynthia Lord (Tweedy) in the North East of England.

CHAPTER IX

❖

THE GUEST CHILDREN

❖

I WISH to mark, by this personal message, my gratitude for the help and kindness which you have shown to the children who crossed the sea from the United Kingdom many months ago. Since the early days of the War, you have opened your doors to strangers and offered to share your home with them. In the kindness of your heart, you have accepted them as members of your own family, and I know that to this unselfish task you and all your household have made many great sacrifices. By your generous sympathy you have earned the true and lasting gratitude of those to whom you have given this hospitality, and by your understanding you have shown how strong is the bond uniting all those who cherish the same ideals. For all this goodwill towards the children of Great Britain, I send you my warmest and most grateful thanks.

Queen Elizabeth asked that this message be sent to every foster family in the middle of the war. It was inscribed inside a decorative border headed by the Royal Coat of Arms in full color. Since Canada had the most plentiful supply of high-quality paper, the message was printed here and sent to families in all the host countries.

Fear, hope and charity brought the guest children to Canada. Fear of bombing and invasion alone persuaded parents to send their children thousands of miles from home. Hope that they would be safe and the parting short made the separation bearable in the early days. But the winter of 1940 ended the hope of a quick return, and parents and children alike came to realize that years of living apart stretched ahead. Charity made the whole scheme work. Thousands of Canadians took in relatives and strangers without expecting payment of any kind. Queen Elizabeth's message of thanks reflected the gratitude felt by many parents and children for the hospitality that was given, on the whole, so freely.

The guest-child program is overshadowed today by the knowledge that the Canadian government refused to help Jewish men, women and children trapped in Hitler's Europe. The same government trampled on the rights of Canadian citizens of Japanese ancestry. Those facts can make a scheme to rescue British children appear as a confirmation of the worst characteristics of Canadian society in the 1940s; certainly, they emphasize its exclusivity, racism and smugly selective conscience. Moreover, the invitation to the guest children was not without political overtones. Crerar's announcement in the House of Commons that Canada had invited ten thousand children to take shelter from the war undercut protests against Prime Minister King's refugee policy. Yet the distinction made by the Immigration Branch between refugees and evacuees kept that same policy intact. The CNCR turned to helping evacuees in 1941 when it became clear that it could not change the government's mind. The story of the guest children would be a more inspiring one today if the welcome had been more open, more generous and less marked by racial and religious barriers.

The evacuation began at a personal level, with appeals from British families to friends and relatives and offers from Canadians to take in the children of people they knew in Britain. The network of connections between British and Canadian families made the danger to children in Britain more personal and vivid to many Canadians than appeals on behalf of European refugees could ever be. For many, it was easier to imagine nieces and nephews trapped in the blitz than strangers threatened by religious and political persecution and the concentration camp. In 1940, also, the idea of a British Empire was still real for many Canadians who wrote and spoke of the "Mother Country" without irony. It was a time when the idea of a British race — so inspiring to Winston Churchill — was still current and respectable. An appeal for homes for evacuees produced thousands of offers. Canada in 1940 was not the country it would become after thirty years of world war, the destruction of empires, liberalized immigration and a conscious commitment to multiculturalism. Mackenzie King ignored the desperate pleas and the generous offer of homes for children from Canada's small Jewish population for fear of offending Quebeckers, and he bowed only reluctantly to pressure from the English-speaking majority to accept evacuees. The number of volunteers even at the height of the enthusiasm, however, was a small part of the population; if ten thousand children had come, it would have been difficult to find them all homes.

The federal government was also reluctant to spend money on the children once they had arrived. It limited its support to travel, hospital care and the cost of administering the scheme. True, it picked up the bill for some evacuees who needed to be subsidized; but successive Ministers of Finance remained vigilantly cost-conscious. The federal government did not pay medical or dental costs, relying instead on the parents to meet those charges. They, in turn, depended on the uncertain willingness of practitioners to treat their foster children without charge for as long as five years. Ottawa left it to the provinces and municipalities to pay the children's education costs. Tax relief was allowed only to foster parents of government evacuees and was never extended to cover private evacuees. When it became clear that fewer than two thousand government evacuees would reach Canada, the government still refused to take responsibility for all evacuees, even though the number was less than the ten thousand invited. Private evacuees had to be in great difficulties before they received government largesse. "Hospitality on the cheap" appeared to be Ottawa's motto.

The guest children did have an effect on childcare agencies in Canada. Communities all across Canada established special evacuee committees to oversee the children's care. In New Brunswick, an entire structure had to be created before the evacuees arrived. In Montreal, a special organization co-ordinated the work of a variety of agencies. Saskatchewan never could afford an adequate organization to care for the children, and relied on one overworked and untrained woman and a network of local committees to do the work. In Alberta, no special efforts were made to oversee the CORB children, and CORB responded by sending few there. Even in those provinces, such as Manitoba, which had a professional body of childcare workers, it was difficult to keep a close watch — as Fred's story plainly demonstrates. Had ten thousand children reached Canada they would have swamped the existing agencies.

The childcare professionals wanted the scheme to prove the value of their methods. They stressed the need for a careful match of child and home and were quick to point out that CORB children in nominated homes were more likely to be moved than those in unnominated ones. This was also true in the United States and was said to prove the value of professional placements.[1] No doubt a good match could produce a happier family, but many of the placements made in 1940 were far from scientific. Workers had limited information about the children. In many provinces, guest homes were approved after a single visit. Sometimes the children spent weeks in the reception centers, giving the staff time to observe them before choosing a home. More often, they were sent to a home within days of their arrival. Difficult cases, usually teenagers, were sent to any approved home willing to have them, and as the supply of homes dried up after 1941, children who needed to be moved were sent to the few homes still available. The bulk of guest children who came to Canada by private arrangements were never matched to their guest homes by any professional standards, yet most of these children stayed with their original family throughout the war. Ten thousand evacuees would have reduced "scientific child placement" to a lamentably bad joke.

The limited number of children helped to make a success of the evacuation. Many middle-aged Canadians can remember a guest child in their community. Some can recall a number of them in the neighborhood or at school and with a little effort can even remember their names. The contrast with the home evacuation program in Britain is striking. British villages and towns were swamped by evacuees. The schools bulged and children attended classes in shifts. Evacuee children often attended their own school with their own teachers in the local school building. Outside the school, the home evacuees formed a separate social group and did little but fight with local children. British people tend to remember "the evacuees" rather than individuals. The guest children, however, rarely appeared in numbers large enough to form separate groups and never in numbers that swamped a local community or its facilities. Widespread criticism of them was unknown during the war.

But Canadians could be a bit stuffy about imagined ingratitude. In 1941, Eddie and Caroline Bell published a memoir of their experiences in Canada and the United States. They called it *Thank you Twice*, which was an allusion to their father's advice that a simple "thank you" was not enough in Canada and America, and they should really lay on the flattery. The book was the witty product of two bright teenagers, and excerpts appeared in *Life* magazine. Some Canadians, however, found the Bells more insulting than amusing and were upset with the pieces. The Toronto University Committee, which had brought the Bells to Canada, passed a resolution declaring that it was not offended by the memoir and the storm soon faded.

Quick absorption into a family helped the guest children through the years in Canada. In Britain, evacuees were billeted with families who had little say in whether or not they wished to be responsible for the children. The children themselves often felt more like lodgers than members of the family.[2] In Canada, this kind of feeling was common only among children in residential schools who spent their holidays as guests of a Canadian family. For the most part, the guest children's very distance from home helped them to form an attachment to their new families. Although they knew that they would eventually return, there were no constant — and painful — reminders of home.

The return to Britain was generally more difficult for the guest children than the first separation and settling in Canada had been. Years divided parents and children. Vera Brittain noted that she seemed to be greeting two young strangers who would have forgotten her completely had they stayed away for two more years.[3] Children joined their foster families as strangers, without expectations; but when they returned to their parents both the children and adults expected something of the family which it could not always rekindle. There were families that soon became as close as ever. But a family with any degree of fragility found it difficult to return to the way things had been in 1940. British habits of childrearing, which insisted on parental discipline over the child and were less concerned with encouraging independence, often led to conflict. School life was torture for most of the returned children, who were plunged into formal, disciplined schools with aloof teachers far removed from the encouraging and helpful staff they had known in Canada. Wartime shortages and restrictions only intensified the difficulties of homecoming.

Those tensions underscored the question many parents must have asked themselves in 1940: "Did we do the right thing?" Early in the war, Anna Freud argued from her wartime work with children that the separation of young children from their parents caused great emotional damage. The evacuations were clearly emotionally damaging, and it is easy to conclude that the children would have been better off at home with their parents.[4] But bombing killed as many children in Britain as were evacuated to Canada, and parents could at least console themselves with the thought that their own children were safe.[5]

In 1945, CORB thought it would be useful to find out how its children had readjusted to British life. The Ministry of Health was not interested. The Minister of Education felt that "the value of the survey to my Department would not justify the work involved," and the suggestion was shelved.[6] There is no study of the effects of overseas evacuation on the children. Obviously, some of the guest children found the move to Canada difficult, the years away from home painful. A number of the former guest children who contributed to this book were surprised by the emotions that surfaced when they sat down to think about their wartime experiences. One man who came to Canada at the age of eleven and returned to settle after the war, looks back on those years as an unhappy time which broke his family "pretty well for good." He writes: "if I was in the same position my parents were in in 1940, I would likely have opted to keep the kids together in England."

Certainly, many guest children were left with a sense of division between families and countries that was never resolved. Overseas evacuation, however, with its emphasis on reconstructing a family for each child, was probably less traumatic than domestic evacuation. For many others, the years spent in Canada can be remembered with pleasure: "I recall the kindness, generosity and understanding that [my] Canadian family showed me and I can't think I was a very rewarding person to have around—young teenagers are not usually and I am sure I was difficult." Another writes: "We shall never forget the overwhelming warmth and generosity of our Canadian welcome at a desolate time for us . . . this wonderful experience strengthens my belief in the importance of international respect and understanding and I am doing my best to see that our children grow up with this attitude." Evacuation also strengthened ties between the branches of some families and between family and foster family: "If one can say that something good came out of the war, I would say in this instance it is the love and friendship that has grown between our families." One man, aged thirteen when he first came to Canada, sees in his evacuation "my biggest break. I shudder to think what I might be doing now if this hadn't happened." A woman, now happily settled in Canada and the mother of three children, has watched "each one reach 9, 13 [and] wondered if I would be as unselfish as my parents and foster parents and the many others in both countries, so placed."[7] Easy generalizations melt away in the light of hundreds of individual lives. In 1940, the children's parents took a risk that their children would be better off in Canada than at home. Nearly fifty years later, the guest children must answer for themselves whether that risk was worth taking.

Abbreviations

Q	Questionnaire
M	Memoir
L	Letter
D	Diary
C	Correspondence with author
I	Interview with author

PAC	Public Archives of Canada
PRO	Public Record Office, London, England
BC	Public Archives, British Columbia
MAN	Public Archives, Manitoba
ONT	Public Archives, Ontario
SASK	Public Archives, Saskatchewan
ONT MIN CSS	Ontario Ministry of Community and Social Services

FCB	F.C. Blair
ALJ	A.L. Jolliffe
HC	Canadian High Commissioner, London
HCUK	British High Commissioner, Ottawa
GM	Toronto, *Globe and Mail*
TES	*Times* Educational Supplement, London

Unattributed quotations are from respondents who do not wish their names to appear. Quoted material has been left unaltered, with the exception of spelling, which has been modified for consistency throughout the text, and punctuation, some of which has been added for the sake of clarity.

Footnotes

Chapter I — The Door Opens

1   Richard A. Titmuss, Problems of Social Planning, History of the Second World War (London HMSO, 1950). Carlton Jackson, *Who Will Take Our Children?* (London, Methuen, 1985). Travis L. Crosby, *The Impact of Civilian Evacuation in the Second World War* (London, Croom Helm, 1986), discusses the strategic considerations behind evacuation planning.

2   BC Add MSS 499 NSCW Scrapbook.

3   8/9/39 PAC MG24J vol. 415 file 3996; Marsh PAC RG 76 vol. 448 file 677774 micro C-10324.

4   1/12/39 F.J. Ney circular PAC MG30 D245 vol. 13.

5   Gerald E. Dirks, *Canada's Refugee Policy* (Montreal, McGill-Queen's, 1977), pp. 62-63; Harold Troper and Irving Abella, *None is Too Many* (Toronto, Lester & Orpen Dennys, 1982), passim.

6   20/7/39 Memo FCB PAC MG26 J4 vol. 205 file 1960 micro C-4279.

7   20/7/39 memo FCB ibid., secret 21/7/39 Constance Hayward—J.P. Thompson, U. of Sask. Presidential Papers series II B-132 (1); 24/7/39 CH-JPT ibid.

8   4/10/39 E.H. Coleman—T.A. Crerar PAC RG 76 vol. 448 file 677774 micro C-10324.

9   16/7/42 HC Debates 3 Sess. 19 Parl. 1942 Vol. 4, 4291.

10   Charles Ritchie, *The Siren Years 1939–45* (Toronto, MacMillan, 1974), pp. 53-54, 57, 60.

11   28/6/40 Montreal *Gazette;* Bruce PAC RG7 G26 vol. 118 file 2085-C.1; CIL MAN RG5 G4 Box 29; Eugenics PAC RG76 vol. 459 file 701110 pt. 1, micro C-10399; 6/7/40 TES; U. of Toronto archives B68/0002/001.

12   25/6/40 J.A.R. Marriott; 29/6/40 Leeson *Times;* 29/6/40 TES; 300 27/6/40 P.M. Heywood—R.A. Wiseman PAC MG30 D245 vol. 13; 9/7/40 PMH—H.V. Stuart ibid., 4/7/40 Heywood—Alvarez ibid.

13   Shakespeare to HC 3/7/40, 6/7/40 TES; 22/6/42 FCB—R. Wallace PAC RG76 vol. 452, file 692762 pt. 1, micro C-10326; 16/6/42 FCB—Graham F. Towers PAC RG 76 vol. 452 file 692762 pt. 1 micro C-10326.

14   L. Wally O'Brien.

15   31/5/40 memo PAC MG20 D245 vol. 13; 27/6/40 Athlone—Sir A. Hardinge PAC RG7 G26 vol. 118, file 2085 C.1; 23/8/40 P.M. Heywood— H.V. Stuart PAC MG20 D245 vol. 13; 29/6/40 HC—Ext. Affs. PAC MG26J1 vol. 292 p. 247204; 4/7/40 O.D. Skelton memo PAC RG25 G2 file 622-40 pt. 1.

16   18/5/40 SS Ext. Affairs—HC PAC MG26J1 vol. 292 p. 247066; 25/5/40 Cabinet War Committee Minutes vol. 1 meeting no. 8 PAC RG27c micro C-4653A. King Diaries 24/5/40.

17   PAC MG26J1 vol. 292 p. 247085; 26/5/40 SS Ext. Aff.—HC ibid.; 28/5/40 FCB memo PAC RG76 vol. 448 file 677774 micro C-10324; 29/5/40 Montreal *Gazette.*

18 31/5/40 *Times;* 31/5/40 memo of meeting in Dominions office PAC MG30 D245 vol. 13; 1/6/40 HC — Ext. Affs. PAC RG76 vol. 438 file 661315 pt. 2 micro C-10316; 5/6/40 PAC MG26J1 vol. 292 p. 247119 micro C-4572; 8/6/40 Ext. Affairs — HC p. 246132; 8/6/40 ibid., p. 246134.

19 Interdepartmental Committee on the Reception of Children Overseas CMD 6213 Brit. Sess. Papers HC 1939-40, vol. 5; Geoffrey Shakespeare, *Let Candles be Brought In* (London, Macdonald, 1949), p. 245.

20 Shakespeare, pp. 247-249; Marjorie Maxse, History of CORB, typescript, PRO DO 131/43 XC/A/045861 p. 5; 20/6/40 *Times;* Vera Brittain, *England's Hour* (London, Futura Books, 1981), p. 55.

21 25/6/40 *Times;* Shakespeare, p. 251, 254; 15/8/40 K. Jopson — CORB PAC RG76 vol. 453 file 693830 micro C-10327; 14/7/40 HC — Ext. Affs. PAC RG76 vol. 438 file 661315 pt. 4; Maxse p. 9; 25/6/40 TAC — HC PAC MG26J1 vol. 292 p. 247189 micro C-4572.

22 29/6/40 *New Statesman;* Maxse, p. 38; PRO DO 131/29.

23 Shakespeare, p. 265; Can HC Debates 1 Sess. 19 Parl. 1940 vol. II 1159-60; 28/6/40 Montreal *Gazette;* 28/6/40 Ext. Affs. — HC PAC RG25G2 file 622-4 pt. 1.

24 Erich Koch, *Deemed Suspect* (Toronto, Methuen, 1980), pp. 59-64; 1/8/40 G.F. Davidson — Isobel Harvey BC RG883, Box 2, file 20; 10/7/40 Dominions Affs. — Ext. Affs. PAC RG25G2 file 622-40 pt. 1; 12/7/40 GM.

25 17/7/40 *Times;* 18/7/40 Montreal *Gazette;* 6/7/40 *Times;* Martin Gilbert, *Winston Churchill vol. VI, Finest Hour 1939-41* (Boston, Houghton Miflin 1983), pp. 670-671; 19/7/40 *Times;* Gilbert p. 671.

26 20/7/40 Montreal *Gazette;* 15/9/41 FCB — C. Cornier PAC RG76 vol. 456 file 694657 pt. 1 (describing policy adopted Aug. 1940).

27 10/7/40 FCB — F.J. Ney PAC RG76 vol. 438 file 661315 pt. 4; 14/7/40 Ney-Massey PAC MG30 D245 vol. 13; Ney PAC RG7G26 vol. 118 file 2085 C.1; 19/7/40 P.M. Heywood — H.V. Stuart PAC MG30 D245 vol. 13; 17/4/42 HCUK — FCB PAC RG76 vol. 452 file 692762 pt. 1 micro C-10326 (re Pembury Grove; Sherborne). In 1942, the British Treasury allowed funds to be sent from British accounts to the schools which had evacuated before July 1940. The schools were St. Hilda's; Byron House; PNEU (Miss Tovey); Roedean; Abinger Hill; Benenden; Pembury Grove; Sherborne. In 1944 all schools were allowed to receive funds from Britain. 17/4/42 HCUK — FCB PAC RG76 vol. 452 file 692762 pt. 2 micro C-10326; 2/4/44 HCUK — ALJ PAC ibid.

28 Shakespeare, p. 256; BC GR 297 Box 10.

29 Q. Mary Ann Hodgson; Phyllis Varah; Elaine Cass; Paul Tinkler in 28/4/84 Victoria *Times Colonist;* BC RG297 Box 16.

30 Q. Malcolm Joyce; 3/10/40 Memo Major Unwin Simson — V. Masey PAC RG25G2 file 622-40 pt. 2, D. Bill Hughes; Q. George Glasper.

31 D. Bill Hughes; 19/8/40 *Times;* Shakespeare, p. 257.

Chapter III — The Door Closes

1 D. H.W.L. Weir; Q. Elspeth Colebrook; J. Middleton-Stewart; L. David Brown.

2 D. Cynthia Jenkins; L. Betty Wilson, Q. Michael Spofforth; Q. Elspeth Colebrook; Q. Rita Thompson.

3 Q. J. Middleton-Stewart; Cynthia Jenkins; H.W.L. Weir; Joyce Barkhouse.

4 Q. Nina Cossins; L. John Spooner.

5 30/8/40 H.E. Davidson—ALJ PAC RG76 vol. 453 file 693830 micro C-10327; 23/8/40 E.P. Kirkwood—E.H. Guston PAC RG30 vol. 8310 file 3070-48-5; 23/9/40 KJ-DG CORB PRO DO 131/45.

6 Q. A.J. McPherson; D. Bill Hughes; Q. V.C. Mann, Phyllis Varah.

7 8/7/40; 20/8/40 GM; Q. Joyce Barkhouse, Peter Victor Gurney, Paddy O'Brien, J. Middleton-Stewart; Donald Stephen Chandler.

8 5/8/40 T.P. Devlin memo PAC RG30 vol. 8340 file 3070-48-2; 26/8/40 memo PAC RG30 vol. 8310 file 3070-40-5; 3/7/40 GM; 5/8/40 Montreal *Gazette*.

9 3/9/40 *Times;* Shakespeare, p. 257.

10 Richard Collier, *1940: The World in Flames* (Harmondsworth, Penguin Books, 1980), pp. 241-247; 23/9/40, 27/9/40 GM; 23/9/40 *Times;* Shakespeare, pp. 272-274; PRO DO 131/20; 3/10/40 *Times;* Maxse p. 6.

11 17/2/41 Jopson memo PAC MG30 E256 vol. 18; TAC statement HC Debates 3 Sess. 19 Parl. 1942 vol. 4, 4291.

Chapter V — An Uncertain Adventure

1 7/10/43 E.H. Blois—GFD PAC RG76 vol. 453 file 693830 NS micro C-10327.

2 For the home children see Joy Parr, *Labouring Children* (Montreal, McGill-Queen's U.P., 1980). 23/12/39, 15/1/40 CW—R.E. Mills PAC MG28 I10 vol. 91 series C-10; memo CW 1939 PAC RG76 vol. 448 file 677774 micro C-10324; CWC Report of Committee on Child Refugees PAC MG28 I10 vol. 89 file C.1(d).

3 Dr. Fred McKinnon, typescript in author's possession; Patricia T. Rooke and R.L. Schnell, *Discarding the Asylum* (Lanham, Md., U. Press of America, 1984), pp. 239-50.

4 29/3/40 CW-Elsie Lawton PAC MG28 I10 vol. 89 file C.1(g); 19/5/40 CW—Constance Hayward PAC MG28 v 43 vol. 4 file 31.

5 6/11/39 IH- CW PAC MG28 I10 vol. 89 file C.1 (g); CWC Report 1940.

6 CW—George F. Mutton, 26/6/40 CW—H.R. Thornber PAC MG28 I10 vol. 88; draft agreement PAC RG76 vol. 458 file 698304 micro C-10399; 8/7/40 Report Dominion—Provincial Conference PAC MG28 I10 vol. 90 file 1866.

7 Rooke and Schnell, p. 359; Minute Books NAC PAC RG76 vol. 453 file 693670 pt. 2.

8   2/10/40 I.D. Griffith —TAC, 18/11/40 M.J. Cullen memo, 11/12/40 ATP—
    FCB, 22/2/41 GFD—FCB PAC RG76 vol. 458 file 698304 micro
    C-10399; 29/3/41 NAC Minutes PAC RG76 vol. 453 file 693670 pt. 2.

9   5/11/40 Shakespeare minute, 30/12/40 Maxse minute, 23/4/41 Snow-
    Maxse, 24/3/41 KJ—Maxse, 24/4/41 DO-HCUK, 17/4/41 Snow—
    Maxse PRO DO 131/13; 27/5/41 Guardianship Bill PRO DO 131/12;
    31/3/42 FCB—Patrick Duff PRO DO 131/13.

10 Charlotte Whitton, "Children on Loan," National Conference of Social
    Work Proceedings (1941), pp. 219-233; 18/2/41 K. Jopson—CORB PRO
    DO 131/47; 17/4/44 Maxse Report PRO DO 131/33; Alberta see Patricia
    T. Rooke and R.L. Schnell, "Charlotte Whitton meets 'The Last Best
    West,'" *Prairie Forum*, 6:2 (1981) p. 150; 28/6/40 Lillian Thomson—CW
    PAC MG30 E256 vol. 18; Saskatchewan 6/6/40 CW—Stewart McKer-
    cher, 6/6/40 CW—Dan H. Young PAC MG28 I10 vol. 89 file C.1(e);
    14/6/40 F.C. Cronkite—CW U. of Sask. FCC Papers Box 1611, 26/9/40
    K. Jopson—Maxse, 25/9/40 GFD—W.A. Doyle PRO DO 131/45;
    10/7/40 Conference re Guest Children Sask. Legis. Assembly Office
    S236; 25/9/40 GFD—K. Jopson PRO DO 131/45; Maxse Report;
    18/1/45 APP—ALJ PAC RG76 vol. 453 file 693830 Sask. micro C-10327.

11 Dr. Fred McKinnon, typescript; 18/2/41 K. Jopson—CORB PRO DO
    131/47, 25/6/40 PAC RG76 vol. 456 file 694687 pt. 1 micro C-10398.

12 7/10/40 IH Report on overseas children BC GR883 Box 2 file 21; Betti
    Sandiford Report U of T B68 0002/004; McKinnon, typescript; On-
    tario 1069, 693, 533 misc. 317. Masons 158, Rotary 20, Eugenics Soci-
    ety 36, PAC RG76 vol. 453 file 693830 Ont. micro C-10327; 30/8/43
    ATP—ALJ PAC RG76 vol. 472 file 725982 pt. 1.

13 Special Report BCG p. 7 PAC RG76 vol. 453 file 693830 Ont; Ont.
    Dept. of Public Welfare Annual Report 1940-41 p. 8; 7/10/40 IH Report
    on OC BC GR883 Box 2 file 21; Dept. of Health and Public Welfare
    Annual Report MAN RG5 G4 Box 28, MAN RG5 G4 Box 34; 3/8/40
    GM reported that 56,845 places were offered but 30,585 needed some
    help.

14 22/6/40 Sexton—GFD 24/6/40 GFD—Sexton BC GR883 Box 2 file
    19; Memo MAN RG5G4 Box 28; agreement PAC RG76 vol. 453 file
    693830 Sask.; Guest Child Conf. Sask. Legis. Assembly S236; Maxse
    History p. 24; Special Report BCG p. 7 PAC RG76 vol. 453 file 693830
    Ont., Maxse History p. 25; 17/2/41 Conference re movement of refugee
    children PAC MG30 E256 vol. 18; 29/10/41 IH—Fred McKinnon BC
    GR883 Box 2 file 32; MAN RG5 G4 Box 35; BC GR297, Box 9; 4/11/40
    Jopson—CORB PRO DO 131/45.

15 25/9/40 GFD—V.A. Doyle PAC RG76 vol. 458 file 693830; 2/9/40
    TRB—Jopson 5/9/40 Jopson—TRB PRO DO 131/45; Montreal 21/8/40
    AGF—FCB, 30/9/40 AGF—GFD PAC RG76 vol. 456 file 694687 pt.
    1 micro C-10398; Blois PAC RG76 vol. 45 file 693830 NS micro C-10327;
    Maxse, History, p. 24.

16   25/7/40, 27/7/40 G.F. Amyot – J.J. Haegerty; 9/8/40 memo PAC RG76, vol. 452 file 693248 micro C-10326; John Stevenson, *British Society 1914-45* (Harmondsworth, Penguin, 1984), p. 204; GFD memo PAC RG76 vol. 452 file 693248 micro C-10326; 7/8/40 BOC Minutes U of T B68 0002/001; Maxse, History; rejection 8.16% on inspection, dock side rejection raised the rate to 8.73%, 11/3/41 HBJ memo; 20/8/40 HBJ – C.F. Brown, 9/9/40 FCB memo, 13/9/40 FCB – TAC, 11/9/40 FCB – CFB PAC RG76 vol. 452 file 693248 micro C-10326.

17   Q. & L. N. Spence; MAN RG5G4 Box 45.

18   Q. Adam McPherson; "Evacuees, 1940" Molly Hyndman, typescript.

19   Q. Phyllis Varah; Q. Joyce Barkhouse; L. Patricia James; Q. Mike Cottrill; lice BC GR297 Box 11.

20   BC GR297 Box 21; 14/1/40 PRO DO 131/95; Q. Jean Gilkes; Q. Joyce Barkhouse; Ont. Min. CSS BCG series; MAN RG5 G4 Box 44.

21   Q. Donald Chandler; Q. Peter Gurney; Q. Dorothy Hynes; Gladys Simmons; Q. Dudley Meech; Ont. Min CSS BCG; MAN RG5 G4 Box 45. The conclusions are drawn from responses to Q.

22   Q. George Glasper; Q. Phyllis Varah; Q. N. Spence; Ont. Min. CSS BCG; MAN RG5 G4 Box 39.

23   MAN RG5 G4 Box 33; August 1940 Morley Luke – F & J Brown (private letter).

24   Q. Yolande Smith; Q. Timothy Leone; Q. Jean Gilkes, Q. Rita Thompson; August 1940 Morley Luke – F & J Brown; Q. Patricia James.

25   Q. & L. N. Spence.

26   Maxse, History, p. 38; 3/11/40 PRO DO 131/45; 19/8/40 E.H. Blois – FCB PAC RG76 vol. 438 file 661315 pt. 5; 5/2/41 Freda Held – B.W. Heise, Ont. Min. CSS BCG; 28/11/40 Minute to Maxse, 28/11/40 Minute from Maxse PRO DO 131/56; 31/3/41 KJ – MM Blair "was really instrumental in putting this through" PRO DO 131/56. 451 of 4596 sent for winter clothes was spent PRO DO131/29; Maxse, History, pp. 38-39.

27   Charlotte Whitton, "Giving outright on $250 a year," *Saturday Night*, 12 April 1941; 6/1/41 H.C. Hebert – Immigration Branch PAC RG76 vol. 456 file 694687 pt. 1 micro C-10398; 1/10/40 BOC minutes vol. 1 U of T B68 0002/001; 22/7/40 HC Debates 1 Sess. 19 Parl. 1940 vol. II 1825-26; 3/4/41 Cab. War Committee Minutes PAC RG2 7c micro C-4653A.

28   20/11/40 ATP – FCB PAC RG76 vol. 453 file 693830 Sask. micro C-10327; Maxse History p. 27, 32.

29   10/1/41 IODE Report MAN RG5G4 Box 29, 17/12/41 IODE Report PAC RG76 vol. 456 file 694687 pt. 1, 15/7/42 IODE Report PAC RG76 vol. 456 file 694687 pt. 2 both micro C-10398; 25/4/41 Ann. Rep. Family Division COS PAC RG76 vol. 456 file 694687 pt. 1 micro C-10398.

30   29/3/41, 30/5/41 Nat. Ad. Committee minutes; 14/11/40 FCB Memo PAC RG76 vol. 456 file 694687 pt. 1 micro C-10398; 9/12/41 FCB – G.W. Coghlin ibid.; Ont. Dept. of Public Welfare Annual Report shows 150 private evacuees under supervision in 1940.

31 4/9/40 Nat. Ad. Committee minutes; 28/8/40, 5/9/40, 17/10/40, 25/10/40 GM; 23/11/40 TES.

32 Stevenson, *British Society,* pp. 245-258; Rebecca Coulter, "The Working Young of Edmonton," in Joy Parr (ed.) *Children and Family in Canadian History* (Toronto, McClelland and Stewart, 1982), p. 146; Robert Stamp "Canadian High Schools in the 1920s and 1930s: The Social Challenge to Academic Tradition," *Historical Papers,* CHA 1978, pp. 76-94; R. Stamp, *The Schools of Ontario 1876-1976* (Toronto, for U of T Historical Studies Series, 1982).

33 Q. Peter Hammill; Q. Gladys Wilson; Q. George Glasper; L. Patricia James; Q. Phyllis Varah; Molly Hyndman typescript (re Duncan and Adam); Q. Tina Howell; Q. Yolande Smith; Q. Elspeth Colebrook; Q. Mike Cottrill; Q. Joyce Barkhouse; Q. Adam McPherson; Q. Donald Chandler; Q. Tony Curtis.

34 St. Hilda's, Archdeacon G.F. Banks typescript; 14/9/40 Sister Elsa O.H.P. circular letter to parents; Lady Eden's, L. & Q. Grania Weir; 30/6/41 P.S. Dobson circular letter; Eric Dennis, "The Roedean Girls," *Chronicle Herald* Halifax, 1981; 27/4/42 D. Reader-Harris—Major Ney PAC MG30 D245 vol. 13.

Chapter VII — For the Duration

1 MAN RG5 G4 Box 45.

2 Ont. Min. CSSBCG; MAN RG5 G4 Box 39, 43; BC GR297 Box 10.

3 L. J.A. Jarvis; 27/12/1940 Yorkshire *Post;* Molly Hyndman typescript; Q. Dudley Meech; Q. Jean Gilkes; 3/4/41 David Brown—Mrs. F. Brown; Q. Min Hunter; Q. Judith Beard.

4 Q. Dudley Meech; 23/8/43 EHB—ALJ PAC RG76 vol. 472 file 725982 pt. 1; 24/11/43 D.S. Archdale—ALJ PAC RG76 vol 473 file 725982 pt. 2; 23/9/43 ALJ—N.E. Sanders MAN RG5 G4 Box 29; 7/12/43 A.P. Phin—ALJ PAC RG76 vol. 453 file 693830 Sask. micro C-10327. Sask. payments ran from $5—$10 a month usually for older children or homes with limited means.

5 1/2/41 GFD memo PAC RG76 vol. 452 file 693670 pt. 1 micro C-10326; 15/9/41 J.M. Byers memo PAC RG76 vol. 456 file 694687 pt. 1 micro C-10398; 12/12/41 JMB—FCB; 10/2/44 JMB memo ibid.; ALJ—J. Gregoire PAC RG76 vol. 456 file 694687 pt. 2 micro C-10398.

6 8/8/41 EHB—CW PAC MG28 I10 vol. 92 series C.11; 4/12/41 BOC Minutes vol. 1 U of T B68 0002/001; MAN RG5 G4 Box 28; McKinnon typescript; Report on Overseas Children MAN RG5 G4 Box 28; 17/11/41 Asst. Director Child Welfare—Dr. F.W. Jackson MAN RG5 G4 Box 30; 7/5/42 BOC Minutes vol. II U of T B68 0002/001; 27/10/42 B.W. Heise—A.P. Pullan Ont. Min. CSS BCG; Maxse Report; 12/3/41 K. Jopson—B.W. Heise Ont. Min. CSS BCG; 10/9/42 BOC Minutes vol. II, U of T B68 0002/001.

7   25/2/42 EHB — FCB PAC RG76 vol. 453 file 693830 N.S. micro C-10327; BC GR297, Box 19; MAN RG5 G4 Box 42; Ont. Min. CSS BCG.

8   Ont. Min. CSS BCG; BC GR297 Box 3; Sept. 1943 Circular to CAS Ont. Min. CSS BCG.

9   10/4/42 FCB — EHB PAC RG76 vol. 453 file 693830 N.S. micro C-10327, Maxse, History, 20/4/43 Maxse — Archdale PRO DO 131/39; E. Harmer — Maxse PRO DO 131/38; 17/6/43 HCUK circular Cmd. 2 975H/296 MAN RG5 G4 Box 29. To January 1944 56 CORB returned, 1944 222 returned Maxse, History, pp. 35-37; Dept. of Mines and Resources Annual Report 1944-45, p. 197 shows 73 CORB in Canadian forces; 555 returned after November 1944.

10 Q. Olive Blythe; Q. Patricia James.

11 Maxse, History, p. 50; Carlton Jackson, *Who Will Take Our Children?*, p. 169; 15/11/43, 13/9/43, 7/12/43, 8/2/44, 14/3/44, 13/11/44 U of T WWSC U of T B68 0002/004; for descriptions of WE trip home see Anthony Bailey, *America Lost and Found* (N.Y. Random House, 1980); 8/11/44 ALJ — F.W. Jackson MAN RG5 G4 Box 28.

12 MAN RG5 G4 Box 42; Q. Yolande Smith; Q. Hazel Love; Q. Judith Beard; Q. Chris Lambert; Q. Jean Gilkes; 22/2/46 B. Beaumont memo Ont. Min. CSS BCG correspondence.

13 MAN RG5 G4 Box 42; January 1944 BC GR297 Box 19; Ont. Min. CSS BCG; BC GR297 Box 19.

14 HC Debates 4 Sess. 19 Parl. 1943 vol. 5 4560; PAC RG2 Series 18, Box 70, file D-17-11; of 1535 CORB 1326 returned to U.K. by February 1946; 4 had died including 2 killed in action PRO DO 131/43. In 1945 31 CORB children visited Maxse in London and of these 10 wanted to return to Canada and 10 more would go back if their parents would join them 22/2/46 Maxse memo PRO DO 131/46.

15 BC GR296 Box 6; Q. Tim Leone; Q. Patricia James; Q. Dudley Meech; Q. Mary Ann Hodgson; Q. Jean Middleton-Stewart; Q. Peter Hammill; Q. Gladys Wilson.

16 Q. David Brown; Q. Paddy O'Brien; BC GR297 Box 3; Q. Phyllis Varah; Q. George Clayton; Q. Mary Ann Hodgson; Q. Yolande Smith; Q. Penelope Jacques; Q. Judith Beard.

17 Q. Joyce Barkhouse; Q. Michael Spofforth; Q. Chris Lambert; Q. Mike Cottrill; Q. Malcolm Joyce; Q. Penelope Jacques, Q. Mary Ann Hodgson; Q. Dudley Meech.

18 Q. Don Chandler; Q. Min Hunter; Q. Jean Gilkes; Q. Malcolm Joyce.

Chapter IX — The Guest Children

1   Kathryn Close, *Transplanted Children* (New York: Committee for the Care of European Children, Inc., 1953), p. 10.

2   See Virginia Massey, *One Child's War* (London: Ariel Books, 1978); Crosby. Impact discusses the hostility many host communities developed toward evacuees.

3   Vera Brittain, *Testament of Experience* (London: Victor Gollancz, 1957), pp. 316, 323.
4   As Carlton Jackson does in *Who Will Take Our Children?*
5   7736 killed, Close, p. 23. 7731 children were evacuated to Canada 1939-41.
6   30/10/45 Ellen Wilkinson—John Parker M.P., PRO DO 131/70.
7   Anthony Bailey, *America Lost and Found*. L. Patricia James; Q. Elspeth Colebrooke; Q. Joyce Barkhouse; L. Betty Milne.

Bibliography

Anthony Bailey, *America Lost and Found* (New York, Random House, 1980).

Caroline and Eddie Bell, *Thank you Twice* (New York, Harcourt Brace, 1941). Written by two children evacuated to Toronto who subsequently moved to the U.S.A.

Vera Brittain, *England's Hour* (London, Futura Books, 1981).

------------, *Testament of Experience* (London, Victor Gollancz, 1957).

Kathryn Close, *Transplanted Children* (New York, US Committee for the Care of European Children, 1953).

Travis L. Crosby, *The Impact of Civilian Evacuation in the Second World War* (London, Croom Helm, 1986).

Gerald E. Dirks, *Canada's Refugee Policy* (Montreal, McGill-Queens, 1977).

Carlton Jackson, *Who Will Take Our Children?* (London, Methuen, 1985).

B.S. Johnson (ed.), *The Evacuees* (London, Victor Gollancz, 1968).

Erich Koch, *Deemed Suspect* (Toronto, Methuen, 1980) — concerns internees sent to Canada by U.K.

Joy Parr, *Labouring Children* (Montreal, McGill-Queens, 1980) — treats the earlier juvenile migrations.

Charles Ritchie, *The Siren Years 1939-45* (Toronto, MacMillan, 1974).

Patricia T. Rooke and R.L. Schnell, *Discarding the Asylum* (Lanham, Md., University Press of America, 1984).

Geoffrey Shakespeare, *Let Candles be Brought In* (London, Macdonald, 1949).

Richard A. Titmuss, *Problems of Social Planning; History of the Second World War* (London, HMSO, 1950).

Harold Troper and Irving Abella, *None is too Many* (Toronto, Lester & Orpen Dennys, 1982).

Geoffrey Bilson was born in Cardiff, Wales, in 1938 and grew up in Liverpool, where he spent a lot of time under the stairs during the blitz. He earned his B.A. at the University College of Wales, his M.A. at the University of Omaha, and his Ph.D. at Stanford (1970). Professor Bilson taught history at the University of Saskatchewan from 1964–65, and from 1967 until his death in 1987. He and his wife Beth, a professor of law, had two children, Max and Kate. He is well known for his children's books published by Kids Can Press: *Death Over Montreal* (1982), *Goodbye Sarah* (1982), and *Hockey-Bat Harris* (1984); he also wrote *A Darkened House: Cholera in the 19th Century* (1980), published by the University of Toronto Press, a result of his interest in Canadian medical history. Known for his sense of humor, his modesty, his varied interests, his love of books and old movies, and respected for his dedication to teaching and to literature, Professor Bilson is much missed by his family, friends, and community.